Arabic for
Designers

MOURAD BOUTROS

Arabic for Designers

An inspirational guide to Arabic culture and creativity

193 illustrations

Table of Contents

FOREWORD

Foreword

No designer contemplating working for a client based in the Middle East should leave home without this book.

Those of us who have attempted Middle Eastern projects cannot help but be aware that many aspects of Arabic-speaking cultures remain a mystery to our Western minds and experiences. When it comes to commercial work with paying clients any gaffes due to this knowledge gap can be both embarrassing and expensive.

Arabic for Designers is both informative and entertaining. Informative because it covers the historic and cultural roots of Arabic calligraphy and typography, while also featuring some of the best contemporary examples of these long-standing traditions. Entertaining because it describes the pitfalls and disasters perpetuated by unsuspecting Western designers and ad people.

Such gems include when the folks at Virgin Atlantic printed Arabic gibberish because no one bothered to check the grammar, or sequential frames created for Arabic-speaking markets that don't take into account that Arabic is read from right to left. Believe it or not, such mistakes are still made today!

Given that we designers often use analogies and metaphors to communicate, knowing what not to turn up with at the presentation in Dubai will definitely prevent some embarrassing moments.

Obviously, not every possible cultural gaffe and hysterical spelling mistake is contained in this book. However, it goes a long way to point out where possible mistakes can be made, and also that help is at hand, not just in this book, but also in the person of Mourad Boutros, who is the author and fount of all knowledge when it comes to Arabic for designers.

Martin Lambie-Nairn

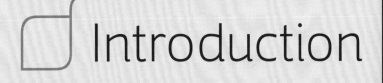

Introduction

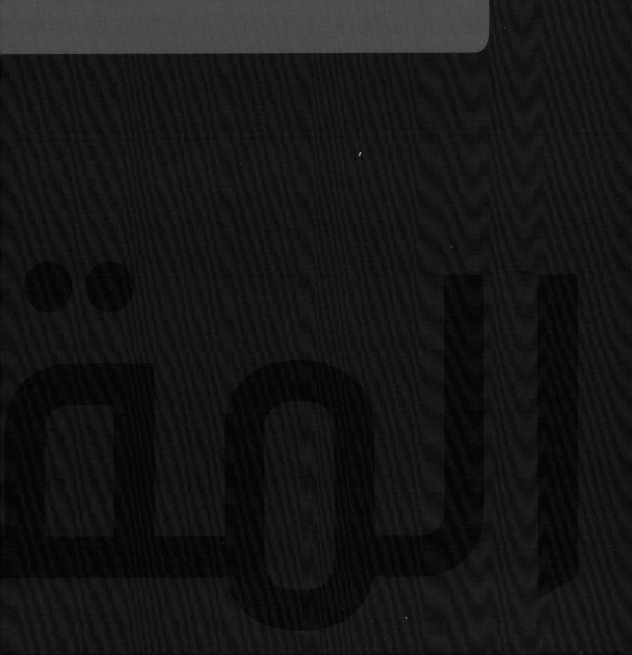

Al tawasol, meaning 'connected', is a collaboration between Mourad Boutros and Alastair Creamer. The piece was one of twenty-six artworks created for '26 Words', which is a collaborative work between 26 (a not-for-profit collective of writers) and Letter Exchange. Writers were paired with visual artists and each pair randomly chose a word to represent each letter of the alphabet.

For Boutros, the task at hand was to have the calligraphy visually translate the richness of the term 'connected', and hence the Arabic language, by showing how both cultures can communicate, connect, and engage in dialogue.

INTRODUCTION

The hybridization and fusing of myriad cultures and economies that define the world today is undeniable, no matter where in the world you call home. But, even as aspects of one culture bend or mould to aspects of another culture, core elements of cultural and national identity remain intact. For individuals, organizations, and companies that endeavour to penetrate a new geographic market from their respective home bases, these long-standing, irrefutable cultural and national tendencies cannot be ignored. In fact, the goal should be to create understanding on the basis of respect in order to best bring disparate cultures together, without forcing the unwanted sacrifice of cultural norms that inform how individuals view their place in the world, which we all share.

An article in *The New York Times* examined the reasons why 'after eight years, Japan is one of a few major countries Google has yet to conquer'. The search engine of choice for most internet users, the Japanese do not use Google with such abandon because when the company first entered the Japanese market, they did so with the same visual look and attitude that had worked for them in the US and Europe. It turns out that the sparse and iconic Google homepage was not to the taste of Japanese internet users, 'who favor sites decorated with a cacophony of text and graphics'. Furthermore, Google Maps and GoogleEarth documented the country's terrain as it had in other parts of the world. But, the realities of narrower streets, a heavy reliance on public transportation hubs, and sensitive historical issues were not taken into account. So, street views actually peered into people's yards, a serious offence in a country that values privacy; directions to a town ended at a geographical centre, and not a train or bus station; 'historical maps … detailed locations of former communities of an "untouchable" caste'. In general, Japanese internet users did not like how Google functioned, so they simply chose not to use it. This case study proves the need to understand and work within cultural parameters, no matter the industry in question or the countries and cultures involved.

It should come as no surprise that the world's relationship with the Arabic language has become more complex since the initial publication of *Arabic for Designers* in 2005. While the acts of extremists in certain parts of the world, from Pakistan and Afghanistan to Syria and France, have fuelled certain stigmas about Arabic-speaking people, the ways in which the Western world has begun to integrate the influx of Arabic-speaking, predominantly Muslim immigrants highlight the critical importance of Arabic in a truly global world.

Worldwide, Arabic is spoken by roughly 295 million people. According to the 2014 Census, approximately 1.1 million Arabic speakers reside in the United States, and in Europe there are approximately fifteen million Arabic speakers. Of all these individuals, a great number of them are also practising Muslims. In England Shariah courts function; in the US, a local bank in Michigan, home to the largest concentration of Arab-Americans in the United States, practises Islamic financial principals.

Conversely, different factions of European governments debate banning the burka, *niqab* and even the building of minarets; in the Middle East 'illegal' fitness centres for women are shut down and teenage students can receive lashes for bringing a mobile phone to school.

Across the globe, tides of understanding and intolerance ebb and flow. The purpose of *Arabic for Designers* is to inform non-Arabic speaking readers, whether they work in global media or multinational business, or just want to learn more about the religious and cultural nuances of Arabic, in the name of bridging understanding.

Variation of nine Arabic characters in one shape

In any language, typography plays a major role in the transfer of information, no matter how horrific the subject matter.

The collection of newspaper front pages reacting to the events of 11 September 2001 marks the beginning of a new era in human history. The Arabic-speaking world was thrust onto centre stage and in a way has not been able to escape the spotlight since then. Of course, an incalculable minority of the planet's Muslim population was responsible for the events in New York City, Washington DC, and Pennsylvania but nonetheless the implications of that day have reverberated throughout Arabic-speaking communities. From Islamic extremists to Jordanian businessmen, the impact of 11 September on the worlds of communication and commerce has reshaped and reframed how these communities view themselves under the scrutiny of the global lens.

As 21st-century readers, these images have been tempered by time and the way we understood them upon their initial publications and the way we understand them now have changed but become no less difficult to frame in a cultural context. The collection of printed reactions to 11 September elicit anger because they strike at the tenets of belief systems many people hold dear, and represent shifts in the political, economic and cultural relevance of Arabic-speaking cultures on a global level.

For all the demographic differences of the world's Arabic-speaking population, it is fair to say that on some level, all these people are consumers of everything from sugar to luxury watches. Aware of the untapped potential of this market, more and more Western businesses have sought to expand brand recognition and convince speakers of Arabic that their brands are the best. Western businesses branching out into Arabic-speaking markets has been going on for years, but in light of 21st-century realities and the accelerated rate at which information is transferred via the internet, the need for Western businesses being able to convert marketing campaigns so they are aesthetically appealing and culturally appropriate for Arabic speakers has increased exponentially. As a direct result of these shifts, Arabic graphic design has also changed, now incorporating elements of Western graphic design.

Arabic for Designers examines the cross-hybridization of Latin and Arabic graphic design approaches. As the book reveals, it is a process that can yield incredibly innovative, beautiful, and successful results. On the other hand, however, without the proper knowledge of the cultural, religious, and linguistic pitfalls of Arabic, advertising and marketing campaigns, not to mention the money invested in such efforts, can be easily lost.

What follows is not a how-to book. Rather, it is a comprehensive look at written Arabic, its calligraphic, typographic, and cultural history, how it has evolved with technological developments from the printing press to digital typefaces, and a colourful and incisive array of examples and case studies that demonstrates how the language functions in multilingual, international marketplaces.

All of these subjects hinge on the idea that language carries the identity of those who speak it and is a formative influence on how those people view the world around them. As the applications of a language change, so too does the identity of its speakers. From its inception as the means to transmit the word of God to its contemporary use to sell tyres and stream real-time news across television and computer screens, Arabic and its speakers find themselves in an era in which they must achieve a balance between tradition and the realities of the contemporary globalized world. In turn, Westerners will also need to have a better understanding of Arabic-speaking populations. Only through mutual understanding and respect can progress be made.

Arabic and English Tanseek Modern letterforms used in '*Qalam*', an exhibition organized by FUNCI (Fundación de Cultura Islámica) in collaboration with the National Library of Morocco in 2010.

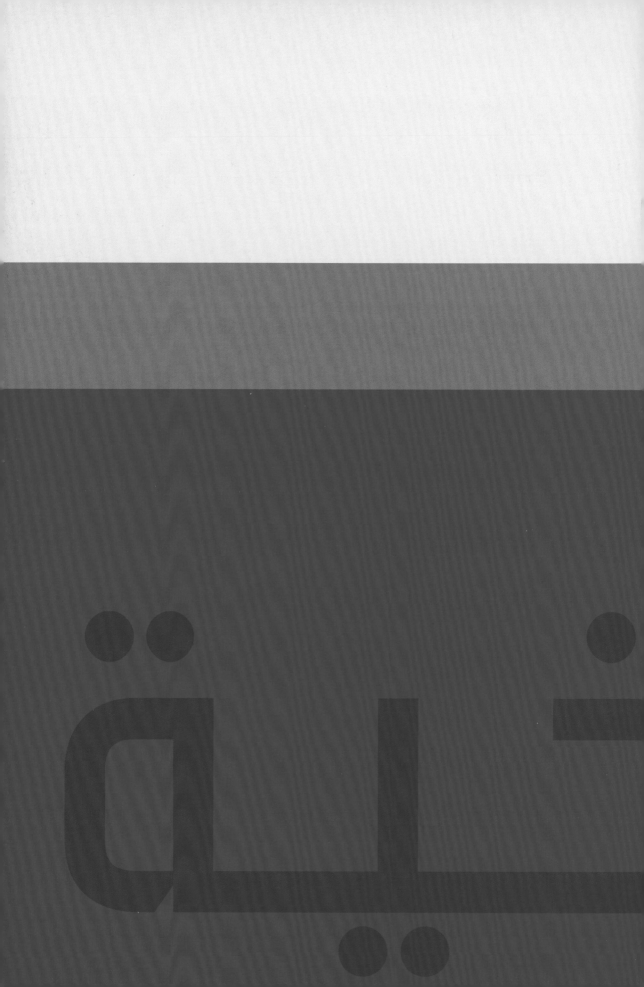

1 Historical Background

Visigothic writing from the 10th century. From *ALPHABETS. a Manual of Lettering for the Use of Students with Historical and Practical Descriptions* by Edward F. Strange, published by G. Bell and Sons, London (1921 edition).

People who speak and read English as a first language do not necessarily understand the historical origins of the language; they also do not always understand the importance of history and culture in the development of all languages, whether English or Arabic. Over time, languages have been spread and imposed all over the world as a result of wars, religion, and commerce. It is fair to say, however, that during the 20th century English secured its position as the world's most important language in terms of global politics and finance. Today, English is the most commonly learned second language across the globe. Before an immersion into the issues and nuances of Arabic, a look into the past will unquestionably provide the tools with which to head into the future.

Germanic in its origin, the English language was brought to Britain by the Jutes, Frisians, Angles, and Saxons, who invaded the island in the 5th century. After the Norman invasion of England in 1066, the English language was extensively enriched by the French language. As a result of speakers of different languages living together, spoken English underwent 'creolization', a linguistic phenomenon that creates a hybrid tongue. Three key events led to the standardizing of the English language, both as it was spoken and written.

First, the Great Vowel Shift changed how vowels were pronounced and marked the transition from Middle English to Modern English (and consequently accounts for English's erratic rules of spelling). Secondly, as more and more documents of business were sent from London to other centres of trade, the official letters were increasingly written in a London-based dialect, which soon became the standard for government missives. Thirdly, and unsurprisingly, the printing press furthered this process of standardizing the language. Due to exploration and colonialism, English spread to the Americas, Asia, Africa, and Australia.

Arabic belongs to the Semitic languages, along with Aramaic and Hebrew, all three of which are read from right to left. Over the course of its history, Arabic spread throughout the world along with the religion of Islam. Today, Arabic is one of the world's most used typographic scripts. In terms of both its history and contemporary applications, the Arabic language can be broken up into two general groups: Classical Arabic and Modern Standard Arabic. Both Classical Arabic and Modern Standard Arabic share a majority of vocabulary, syntax, and morphology, though discernible differences do exist. Classical Arabic is the language of the Holy Qur'an and pre-modern texts, while Modern Standard Arabic is the language of the media and most scholarly and literary texts.

Historically, the last of the Semitic scripts, the Arabic alphabet consists of twenty-eight consonantal signs (three of which are also used as long vowels). Due to the strength of the oral tradition for passing down poetry and literature through the generations, written text was not widespread until the beginning of Islam. In its earliest stages, Arabic writing had no explicit rules as each scriptwriter or calligrapher had his own style of writing. Written Arabic relied on its visual appearance to convey meaning before the actual sentence was read. The shape of script held as much meaning as the content.

Most scholars now agree that the Arabic script, which eventually became the most popular, can be traced back to the Nabataean script dating from the 3rd century. Nabataean script evolved into what became known as North Arabic or North Semitic and further developments produced the static, angular script known as Jazm. It was not until the dawn of Islam in the 7th century that written words, and thus calligraphy, became important.

العلم نور والجهل ظلام

Arabic

ܡܕܥܐ ܢܘܗܪܐ ܘܗܘ
ܗܘܟܠܐ ܚܫܘܟ ܗܘ

Aramaic

חינוך הוא אור בורות היא חושך

Hebrew

'Knowledge is light and ignorance is darkness' written in Arabic, Aramaic, and Hebrew.

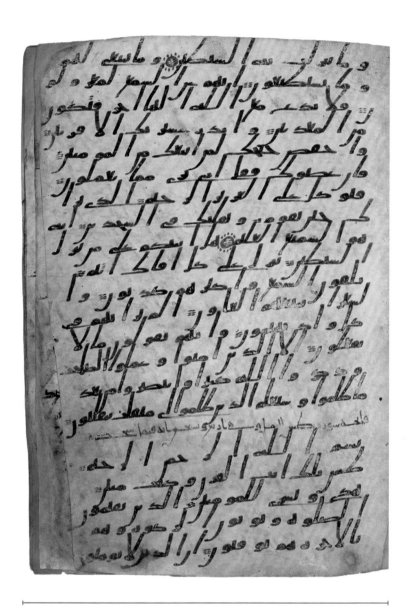

The British Library's oldest Qur'an manuscript: in Mecca or Medina script, 8th century.
Fully digitized and available on the British Library's Digitized Manuscripts site.
Chapter 26, *al-Shu'ara'* (The Poets), verse 183, to Chapter 27, *al-Naml* (The Ant), verse 3

Muslims believe that between the years AD 610 and 632, the Angel Gabriel revealed to Muhammad (PBUH) the Holy Qur'an, a synthesis of the teachings of other prophets, or 'messengers', such as Adam, Noah, Abraham, Moses, and Jesus. Muslims believe that portions of holy texts such as the Torah and the Bible have been forgotten or misinterpreted, while they believe the Holy Qur'an to be the embodiment of perfection that serves as God's final revelation.

The Divine Revelation of Islam created the need to record every word of the Holy Qur'an in exact detail; heroic feats of memory could no longer be relied upon. The Arab fascination with the beauty of the spoken word coupled with the limitations of existing Arabic scripts played a positive role in the development of Arabic calligraphy as an art form. In a relatively short time Arabic script was transformed and beautified. One reason for the aesthetic development of calligraphy was to make it worthy of its status as the sacred script selected by God to transmit His divine message. The other reason for much of the calligraphic innovation during this time was that calligraphy served as a common means for visual expression because figurative art was not allowed under strict interpretations of Islam.

In 651 the first copies of the Holy Qur'an were written in the scripts of Mecca and Medina, local variants of Jazm, but these were soon superseded by Kufic, which took its name from the town of Kufa in Iraq, an early centre of Islamic learning. Approximately 150 types of Kufi script existed in the early history of Arabic's written form, which led to a large amount of variation in the same style. With its origins as a language more often memorized than written, Arabic writing began without any diacritic points. The first radical change that took place in the written language's development was the insertion of diacritic points in the form of red dots on the letters and then a red stroke, which meant different things depending on its positioning: on top (*fatha*) for the sound equivalent to 'a'; on the letter itself for *damma*, for the sound equivalent to 'ou'; and the *kasra* below the line for the sound equivalent to 'e'. Later, Arabic speakers had to use diacritic points to distinguish the different letters of the words to allow non-Arabic speakers to understand and pronounce the phonetics properly and to be able to read the Holy Qur'an. The process was called *Ta'jim* (from the word *Ajam* meaning non-Arabic speakers).

Along with Kufic, many other early cursive scripts were developed but the two most important were Thuluth and Naskhi. Over time, calligraphic developments resulted in the introduction of more new styles, the most important of which was Ta'liq. From the late medieval period to the present day, various derivative scripts have been created to meet particular needs. Among these are Diwani and Riq'a. These early Arabic calligraphic typefaces varied in style because of the scriptwriters' individual tastes and styles.

With the spread of Islam, the need for increased clarity became even more important and various cursive styles gradually came to prominence. Although some of these cursive styles can be traced back to the first decade of the Islamic era, they were mainly used for secular purposes and lacked the elegance and harmony of proportion for which they were later renowned.

Naskhi

One of the earliest cursive scripts, it gained great popularity in the 10th century. Highly legible, it was used for copying the Holy Qur'an. Naskhi is characterized by short horizontal stems and its almost equal vertical depth above and below the medial line. The Naskhi style is widely used today for headings, subheadings, and body copy in newspapers, magazines, books, advertising, and promotional materials. It remains the most widely used of all Arabic styles.

Ta'liq

First developed in Persia during the 15th century, it spread to Turkey and the Indian subcontinent. The word means 'hanging' in Arabic and refers to the fluid cursive style and strokes that vary from thin to thick. Today, it is used in newspapers and magazines in Iran, Afghanistan, and Pakistan where hand-written calligraphy is still common.

Diwani

Based on Ta'liq, but with less dramatic hanging baselines, Diwani evolved in the 16th century in Turkey and is noticeably cursive (top). The decorative version known as Diwani Jali is widely used for ornamental purposes.

Riq'a

Riq'a can be traced back to the 15th century but did not come to prominence until the early 19th century. A derivative of a number of cursive scripts, Riq'a was primarily used for secular purposes and is characterized by its thick rounded curves. Today it is widely used in Egypt under the name of Egyptian Rokaa (bottom), which is wider and more airy than the original.

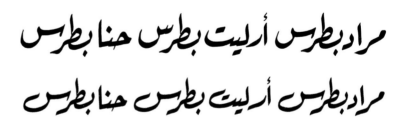

Thuluth

Thuluth can be traced back to the 7th century but did not develop fully until the late 9th century. Thuluth is still regarded as one of the most important of the ornamental scripts and its fluid, thin lines are used for calligraphic inscriptions, titles, and headings.

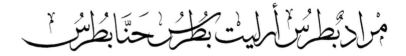

Kufic

Kufic script achieved a level of perfection in the 8th century, resulting in its application as the script used to transcribe the Holy Qur'an. The script is characterized by its static, rectangular lines and the short vertical strokes and extended horizontal lines. Kufic was the dominant Qur'anic script for more than 300 years. Decorative elements and illuminations were added to Kufic texts and the letters developed into purely ornamental forms.

It was the 10th-century calligrapher Abu 'Ali Muhammad Ibn Muqlah who consolidated and standardized the major cursive styles. Ibn Muqlah used his knowledge of geometry to produce a comprehensive system of scientific calligraphic rules. He redesigned the forms of the letters using three standard units: the rhombic dot, the Alif, and the circle. The standard Alif (equivalent to 'A' in the Latin alphabet) was a vertical stroke measuring a specific number of rhombic dots (between six and eight) that varied according to the particular style. The standard circle had a radius equal to the height of the Alif. Ibn Muqlah originated this geometric system and the following generations of calligraphers perfected and beautified its application. These scripts went on to evolve special ornamental forms that began to compete successfully with Kufic.

The harmony of proportion that spoke to the essence of written Arabic in relation to the religion of Islam, and to Arabic-speaking cultures, represents Ibn Muqlah's crowning achievement and is the primary reason his typographic rules have endured history.

Calligraphers hone their skills by measuring the proportions of script against rhombic dots, which are the same in size as the tip of a bamboo calligraphy stick.

Character	Transcription	Character Name	Pronunciation
ا	ā	Alif	long a
ب	b	Bā'	b
ت	t	Tā'	t
ث	th	Thā'	th
ج	dj	Djīm	j
ح	ḥ	Ḥā'	aspired h
خ	kh	Khā'	kh
د	d	Dāl	d
ذ	dh	Zhāl	dh
ر	r	Rā'	r
ز	z	Zāyn	z
س	s	Sīn	s
ش	sh	Shīn	sh
ص	ṣ	Ṣād	dark, unvoiced s
ض	ḍ	Dhād	dark, unvoiced d
ط	ṭ	Ṭā'	dark t
ظ	ẓ	Ẓāh'	dental z
ع	'	'Ayn	glottal fricative
غ	gh	Ghayn	gh
ف	f	Fā'	f
ق	ḳ	Qāf	q
ك	k	Kāf	k
ل	l	Lām	l
م	m	Mīm	m
ن	n	Nun	n
ه	h	Hā'	h
و	(ū) w	Wāw	w or long u
ي	(ī) y	Yā	y or long i

The Industrial Revolution also played an important role in maintaining Ibn Muqlah's methods. The Ottoman Sultans did not explicitly oppose the newly created printing process, but they insisted that it should not misrepresent their script, as many Western typographic attempts did. Arabic calligraphers feared for their jobs and boycotted the rapidly growing printing industry. While Latin typography continued to evolve, Arabic calligraphers isolated themselves and carried on using their pens and bamboo calligraphic sticks. This caused a serious delay in the development of Arabic typography and led to rigidity in contemporary Arabic typefaces, creating problems in bringing Arabic typography in line with other typefaces.

There is an irony here that merits attention: the oldest known documents that contain written Arabic date back to AD 512 and are trilingual, written in Arabic, Greek, and Syriac (a form of Aramaic). The fossilization of Arabic typography was a cultural phenomenon that until relatively recently had been an accepted facet of the culture at large. The fact that a written language that initially embraced multilingual treatments, and then cut itself off from the world, and is in need of realigning with the typographic trends of the rest of the world indicates how language represents culture, not only to the people who speak the language, but also to everyone who does not speak the language.

In light of this self-imposed typographic isolation, it is worth mentioning the story of the Aramaic language in order to best understand the importance of foreign influence, or its lack thereof, on typographic development. In the particular case of Arabic, Aramaic also serves as a perfect example because the two are sister languages, though history has treated them both very differently.

The Bible in Syriac, Amid, Turkey, 463–4. Genesis 29:25–30:2.

Aramaic is really a group of related languages, not a single monolithic language. The two families of Aramaic dialects can be roughly classified as 'Eastern' and 'Western', the Euphrates River being the dividing line. Aramaic is still in use today, mainly for the purpose of rites and rituals in churches, shrines, and other holy places. For this reason, it has never been brought to the forefront of typographic debate as technology has advanced.

The word 'Aramaic' stems from Aram, the fifth son of Shem, the first-born of Noah. The descendants of Aram dwelt in the fertile valley Padan-aram ('between the two rivers'). The Aramaic language in Padan-aram remained pure and developed as the common language for all the Semitic clans: Assyrians, Chaldenians, Hebrews, Phoenicians, and Syrians. By the 8th century BC, it was the most common language from Egypt to Asia Minor to the Middle East.

The language of the people of Palestine shifted from Hebrew to Aramaic sometime between 721 and 500 BC. Therefore, we know that Jesus, his disciples, and their contemporaries spoke and wrote in Aramaic. The message of Christianity spread throughout the Arabian Peninsula in this Semitic tongue. Both the Babylonian and the Palestinian Jewish Talmuds were written in Aramaic. Findings from Egypt in 1900 of Jewish-Aramaic papyri have uncovered many passages in biblical Aramaic. The discovery of the commentary on the Book of Habakkuk in the caves of Qumran in Jordan (also known as 'The Dead Sea Scrolls') further demonstrates how Aramaic has been in constant use from early times to the present day.

Aramaic remained dominant even though Greek had spread widely throughout the region by the 4th century BC. This continued to be the case until Aramaic was largely superseded by her sister Semitic tongue, Arabic, after the Arab conquest in the 7th century. In spite of the pressure from the ruling Arabs to force people to speak Arabic, Aramaic was kept alive domestically, scholastically, and liturgically.

The Maronites, a Christian sect centred in Lebanon, resisted the imposition of the Turkish language after the Ottoman occupation of their land in the late 16th century. They adopted Arabic as a spoken and written language, but they continued to use Aramaic domestically. Today, Aramaic remains the language of their liturgy, as of the liturgy of other Eastern Christian sects in the Near and Middle East.

A living proof of this strong self-autonomy can be found in their churches and shrines. As in all old religions, calligraphy played a holy role in carrying God's words. In the Christian Maronite religion calligraphy was used to illustrate the message of God. That is why we find calligraphy associated with all sorts of religious paintings whether on paper, canvas, or cave wall frescos. Most of the frescos and practically all the paintings carry elements of calligraphy if not large portions of text.

Today, the religious communities still using Aramaic as a liturgical language are the Christian sects of the Jacobites, the Nestorians, the Maronites, the Chaldeans, the Aramaic, the Malabar, the Malankar, and the Armenians. As the result of his research, the outstanding Aramaic and Arabic scholar Professor Franz Rosenthal wrote in the *Journal of Near Eastern Studies* (April 1978):

> In my view, the history of Aramaic represents the purest triumph of the human spirit as embodied in language (which is the mind's most direct form of physical expression) over the crude display of material power. The Aramaic language conquered great empires, and when they disappeared and were submerged in the flow of history, that language persisted and continued to live a life of its own ... The language continued to be powerfully active in the promulgation of spiritual matters. It was the main instrument for the formulation of religious ideas in the Near East, which then spread in all directions all over the world ... The monotheistic groups continue to live on today with a religious heritage, much of which found first expression in Aramaic.

If the history of Aramaic is the fulcrum of a scale off which both Latin and Arabic typography hang, it becomes easy to see how outside forces influence the development of national typographies. Latin typographers, steeped in the excitedly experimental milieu of Renaissance Europe, soon branched out into Arabic, Hebrew, and Asian printing. It was Lebanese scholars working in Europe who contributed importantly to the development of Semitic language typography in Italy, France, and Holland.

As the following chapters reveal, however, the printing press did eventually arrive in the Middle East and with it the desire, and need, to convert a calligraphic language into one that could also be applied typographically.

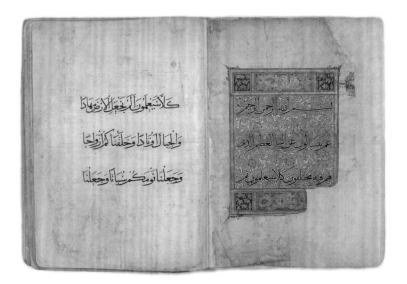

Pages from a Qur'an from Turkey or Iran, 1333. Spencer Collection, The New York Public Library Digital Collections

2 Type Design

Elements of Typography

In the global marketplace, graphic designers are often required to use several languages on the same piece of work. Because different languages occupy varying amounts of space to convey the same information, a great deal of knowledge is required to skilfully manipulate multiple languages, especially when they are not Latin-based scripts. Latin type design developed without any thought to combining and mixing with structurally different scripts like Arabic or Japanese. In a similar way, Arabic typography developed in isolation from say, Latin or Chinese. Current multilingual integration of Arabic, Latin, and other typographies imposes the need for a visual language that reflects individual cultural identities but also speaks to the global community and its wealth of diversity. Given the rigidity of Latin design, Arabic typography has been subjected to a new system of typographic manipulation in order to keep apace with global design trends and expectations.

The difficulty in such an endeavour, however, is that cultural history not only holds the key to the problem, it is in fact the cause of the problem. Making an Arabic typeface that looks like Latin, or can work concurrently with it, is nothing but a surface solution for a real problem that requires more attention from Arabic and Latin users. The quality of newly designed typefaces should reinforce and not undermine the integrity of the culture. Culture is not explicitly expressed in an ideology or a body of doctrines. Rather, it is an activity. Culture is the activity of ordering, disordering, and reordering in the pursuit of understanding and for establishing values, which guide action. As Richard Buchanan observed in the journal *Design Issues* (spring, 1998), 'Culture is the search for principles in the every day engagement of life as well as in the special human engagements of science, art, politics, and design. In short, culture is what we do when we are alone or when we are together in such a pursuit.' Contemporary Arabic typography thrives when it establishes and honours cultural background through actual typographic design.

Before delving into a thorough examination of contemporary Arabic typography and its use in a world heavily informed by Western visual aesthetics, a working definition of typography needs to be established. In doing so, there is an ongoing debate that will never be resolved, though for the purpose of this book it must be raised: can handwriting be considered as typography?

In terms of Arabic, calligraphy should be considered the starting point of typography. It doesn't matter if it is the result of regular pens, pencils, brushes, or bamboo, any handwriting, even if it is not legible, can be classified as calligraphy. In the early history of Arabic two distinct branches of calligraphy existed. Calligraphy as an art (*khatt*), and in turn the calligrapher as an artist (*khattat*), was not the same as calligraphy as copy (*naskh*), and the calligrapher as a copyist (*mustansikh*). As has been discussed, written Arabic was put through a process of standardized mathematical proportioning. As the most commonly applied proportioned script, Naskh became the model for early Arabic type cutters.

Then there is the choice of Arabic calligraphy or Islamic calligraphy. Arabs and non-Arabs all over the world define calligraphy as the art of writing, irrespective of tribal, national, or religious identities. Hence the term 'Islamic calligraphy' is used to avoid the impression that Arabic scripts are only used, and used innovatively, by calligraphers from Arab nations. Arabic calligraphers exist all over the world, regardless of their cultural, national, and religious background. In terms of both forms of calligraphy, however, what they have in common is the fact that both are created by the human hand, which no matter how practised and talented never can be as uniformly precise as physical or digital type. We can say the calligraphy is Arabic, but some calligraphers also use the term 'Islamic ornaments'.

Typography is an applied art; its primary function is to communicate. When we read, the shapes and forms of the letters communicate various meanings. But when we write we also make visible signs. What distinguishes computer type from the most practised handwriting is how it can be precisely and easily replicated. Typography then is the art and technique of selecting and arranging type styles, point sizes, line lengths, line spacing, character spacing, and word spacing for typesetting applications.

What happens when computer technology is used to emulate the variances of handwriting as typography? Bello is one such typeface. So, in the word 'Bello' the two 'l's' are not exactly the same in shape, as is the case in handwriting. Some Western design circles, unfamiliar with the structure of Arabic script, confuse the regular complexity of proportional Arabic typography with such experimental randomizing. Consequently, such issues become the subject of heated, sometimes confused debate, with no definitive answer. Yet they are well worth keeping in mind as the history of Arabic typography is revealed in the light of contemporary applications. It has become the ultimate challenge to type and font designers to produce an authentic Naskh script. The best Arabic type designs are those that care to give back to the reader the pleasure of functional elegance typical of well-written manuscript Naskh.

Designed and created by Marwan Aridi, this page of a Qur'an maintains a traditional look, though it merges many non-traditional elements. The calligraphy embraces elements of Kufi and Diwani, creating a script with elegant ascenders and descenders.

شـركــة بطــرس الـدوليــة للاستشــارات

قامت شـركـة بطـرس الـدوليـة للاستشـارات والتصاميم بابتكـار مجموعـة مـن الخطـوط والزخـارف الـعربيـة،
آخـذة في عين الاعتبـار امكـان تكـيفهـا لتستخدم مـن قبل أجهـزة التنضيد الـعربيـة التصويـريـة والإلكترونيـة،
وتلك الـعـاملـة باللـيزر، لـهدف استعمـالـهـا في تنضيـد النصـوص. مـن كتب ومجلات عربيـة ومـن أهـم التطـورات
الـتي شـهدتـها صنـاعـة الخـط الـعربي على أجهـزة الكمبيـوتر الشخصيـة، دخـول الخـط الـعربي عـالم النشـر
المكتبي والصحفي، ومحـاولـة التطـور مـع التكنـولـوجيا الـغربيـة، بكل مـا فيها مـن تعقيـدات، ومـراعـاة
المحافظـة على تقـاليـد الخـط الـعـربي. إن الـقسم الأكـبرمـن الشـركـات الـعـالـميـة يتعـامل مـع منطـقـة
الشـرق الأوسـط بـنطـق ومفـهـوم جْـاريـن فـقـط. وإذا أخـذنا قسـم الشـرق الأوسـط /إفـريقيا الـذي يتبع
عـادة للـقسـم الـدولـي في هـذه الشـركـات، فإنـه لا يـمثل أكـثرمـن 2 الى 5 ٪ مـن مجمـوع مبيعـات هـذا
الـقسم. وليـس مـن مجمـوع مبيعـات الشـركـات ككل. إن أكـثرالشـركـات المصنعـة لأجهـزة الكمبيـوتر
الشخصيـة وآلات التنضيـد التصـويري والبرامـج، شـركـات أجنبيـة، يضاف الى ذلك الـقرصنـة المنتشـرة
في طـول الـعـالـم الـعـربي وعـرضـه مـن دون أي رادع. لـكل هـذه الأسـبـاب، فإن صنـاعـة الخـط الـعـربي
لن تتطـور إلا على مستوى فردي فـقـط، مـا يعنـي !!!

شـركــة بطـرس الـدوليــة للاستشــارات

شــركــة بطـرس الـدوليـة للاستشــارات

شـركـة بطـرس الـدوليـة للاستشـارات

This table demonstrates a range of font weights. This one in particular was designed as a
special corporate typeface. The examples read: 'Boutros International Consulting'.

The first Holy Qur'an printed with movable type was completed in Venice in 1538. It was not until the early 17th century that the first books printed with movable Arabic type were printed in Europe. These books were not at all popular in the Middle East, mainly because the printed pages were seen as aesthetically inferior to the work of calligraphers. As a result of the historical animosity between Christians and Muslims, distrust and wariness of Western inventions kept the printing press out of the Middle East for nearly 300 years.

Although the use of Arabic metal type was forbidden in the Ottoman Empire until 1726, printing presses were established by Maronite and Orthodox Christians in the late 16th and early 17th centuries. After the Ottoman ban was lifted, printing presses spread throughout the region for both religious and secular texts. Nevertheless, the Holy Qur'an continued to be reproduced either by handwriting or by offset printing.

Regardless of the language, the following terms universally apply to the study and practice of typography:

Type Family: A progression of design weights, with corresponding italics, condensed, expanded, and ornamental styles within a type design. A family can have as few as eight weights. Examples of weights are light, medium, medium italic, bold, bold condensed, bold outline, bold shadow, and bold inline.

Type Font: A set of characters that have a unified design and purpose such as letters, numerals, punctuation, diacritical marks, and symbols. The term 'type font' is synonymous to the term 'character set'. In the context of digitized typography, the term 'font' is the hardware or software carrier of the character set.

Typeface: A single style variation in a type family, such as light, bold, condensed, or outline.

With this very elementary notion of the elements of typography, it is now appropriate to move on to a comparison of Latin and Arabic typography, which will lead to several studies of how the two not only can be used together, but borrow aesthetic tricks from one another.

Latin vs. Arabic Typography

Boutros Arlette Sans (released in January 2016) is softer, rounder, and less austere than the mechanically constructed sans serif typefaces, either Arabic or Latin, designed during the late 20th and early 21st centuries.

- Latin is written and read from left to right.
- Arabic is written and read from right to left.

- Latin Letters stand alone, except in the case of ligatures.
- Arabic is a combination of connected and stand-alone letters.

- Stretching Latin letters destroys the letters, though certain cursive letterforms with tails do not lose meaning when stretched.
- Stretching Arabic letters is decorative and makes for an incredible visual effect because of Arabic's calligraphic nature and the fact that the letters are attached to one another. Rules exist for which letterforms can be stretched.

- Latin has both upper and lower cases, both of which can be italicized.
- Arabic has no uppercase letters; italics, if not designed and executed properly look as if they have been skewed.

- Latin font design is based on the notion of a set of baselines from which heights of ascenders and descenders are established.
- Arabic font design is based on a complex system of measurements per basic letter shape; letters hardly ever sit on the same baseline and their ascenders and descenders are of various lengths.

- Latin ascenders and descenders follow the basic design grid used to develop a typeface, thus making leading more consistent.
- Arabic ascenders and descenders create different leading sequences.

- Each Latin letter has its own shape, and ligatures are included in a font's basic character set, for an alphabet of fifty-two letter shapes divided into two sets of twenty-six letters known as uppercase and lowercase.
- Seven Arabic letters have two shapes and twenty-two letters have four shapes – at the start of the word, in the middle, and at the end, and free standing; eighteen letter shapes are free standing.

- In some European Latin-based languages, accents denote various phonetic sounds and vowels.
- The small accents above or below Arabic letters denote phonetic sounds and soft vowels.

بسط جناحيه

بسط جناحيه

بسط جناحيه

بسط جناحيه

إذا أومأ الحب إليكم فاتبعوه وإن كان وعر المسالك زلق المنحدر. وإذا بسط عليكم جناحيه فاسلموا له القياد وإن كان جرحكم سيفه المستور بين قوادمه. وإذا حدثكم فصدقوه. وإن كان لصوته ان يعصف بأحلامكم كما تعصف ريح الشمال بالبستان. إن الحب إذ يكلل هاماتكم. وهو كما يشد من عودكم. كذلك يشذب منكم الأغصان. وكما يرتقى الى أعالي آفاقكم ويداعب أغصانكم الفضة تميس في ضوّ الشمس. كذلك ينزل إلى جذوركم العالقة بالأرض فيهزها هزا. ويضمكم إلى أحضانه كما يضم حزمة قمح. فيدرسكم لكي يعريكم. ثم يفربلكم فيخلصكم من القشور. ثم يطحنكم فيحيلكم دقيقا أبيض. ثم يعجنكم لتلينوا؛ ثم يسلمكم إلى نار هيكله المقدسة .

إذا أومأ الحب إليكم فاتبعوه وإن كان وعر المسالك زلق المنحدر. وإذا بسط عليكم جناحيه فاسلموا له القياد وإن كان جرحكم سيفه المستور بين قوادمه. وإذا حدثكم فصدقوه. وإن كان لصوته ان يعصف بأحلامكم كما تعصف ريح الشمال بالبستان. إن الحب إذ يكلل هاماتكم. وهو كما يشد من عودكم. كذلك يشذب منكم الأغصان. وكما يرتقى الى أعالي آفاقكم ويداعب أغصانكم الفضة تميس في ضوّ الشمس. كذلك ينزل إلى جذوركم العالقة بالأرض فيهزها هزا. ويضمكم إلى أحضانه كما يضم حزمة قمح. فيدرسكم لكي يعريكم. ثم يفربلكم فيخلصكم من القشور. ثم يطحنكم فيحيلكم دقيقا أبيض. تصيروا الخبز المقدس لمائدة الرب المقدسة.

The Boutros MINI Arabic range of typefaces was created in collaboration with Serviceplan Middle East. The brief was to create a range of Arabic typefaces to be in line and in harmony with the characteristics of the existing MINI Latin range of typefaces.

Arabic typefaces, ranging from headlines to body text types, have been introduced for multiple applications by any range of companies. For all of the progress in Arabic typeface development, however, the ability to create typefaces capable of being relevant in the international marketplace without sacrificing the essence of the Arabic language remains a skill in very high demand. Not all typefaces are well designed and executed, rendering them inferior to the standards of international design.

When it comes to typography, the interdependence of the visual features is subject to coordination and balance according to the respective proportions. Any change will affect this intimate relationship and everything has to be modified accordingly. Arabic needs to be treated with less complexity and rigidity by using a more extroverted approach to dealing with the letterforms. This extroverted approach means that designers using Arabic, whether or not they speak Arabic, should not limit themselves to Arabic-speaking culture for inspiration. Again, the ideas of balance and harmony need to be kept in mind, especially when dealing with multilingual texts.

With that said, it is worth mentioning that in the case of advertising materials, good copywriting can overcome this issue in the sense that copy is written and edited to fit the space provided. All over the world countries such as Lebanon, United Arab Emirates (UAE), Egypt, Turkey, the United States, and parts of Canada and China use bilingual or trilingual texts. Historically speaking, one of the most famous examples of a single text incorporating multiple languages was the Polyglot Bible of Christopher Plantin. Published in 1572, Plantin's Bible contained Latin, Greek, Hebrew, Syriac, and Aramaic (though the Aramaic was written in Hebrew characters). In Plantin's Bible the type size, kerning, and leading vary from one language to another but if you compare two opposite pages, they are perfectly balanced visually. In graphic designer Ellen Lupton's words, the Plantin Bible results 'in an overall classicism, which reflects the tastes of the period'. Plenty has changed in 500 years and Arabic typography must continually realign itself with the 'tastes of the period'.

Technology's Role in Typeface Development

What follows is a brief chronology of typesetting methods since the advent of the printing press. It is by no means an exhaustive history. But the only way to clearly understand the present state of Arabic typography and the methods of its application, we need to establish a sense of the past. What has become clear is that over time, the steps required to create new typefaces have become fewer and easier. Whether using metal or malleable materials like plastic, there has been more room to innovate typeface designs the world over.

For nearly 400 years after Gutenberg invented printing, type was set by hand. It was not until the 19th century that typesetting machines were developed. Though there were many variations on the idea of automating the process of composing metal type, only a few became widely used.

Linotype, Intertype, and Ludlow machines cast slugs in fully spaced lines. Monotype machines cast individual pieces of type in justified lines. Invented in 1886 by Ottmar Mergenthaler, Linotype was short for 'a line of type'. Linotype machines used keyboards that set matrices that were cast into a slug (a solid piece of metal). Monotype also utilized a keyboard but the process required two machines. First, a keyboard was used to perforate a ribbon or strip of paper with the chosen letters and characters. The ribbon or paper was then run through a machine that cast the type.

The next major development that influenced how type was set came in 1949 with the advent of photographic typesetting. A photographic line-composing machine produced justified copy on film and photographic paper. The luxury of direct image composition, the ability to combine type with images, reduced the number of steps required during production and allowed for entire pages to be composed replete with images.

The Fontek Collection from
Letraset
Decorative *Script Fonts*
Fonts **Sans Serif Fonts**
Serif Fonts

The Fontek Collection from Letraset is an extensive collection of typefaces to meet any design requirement, from classic to contemporary, retro to revival.

Boutros Advertisers Naskh (in eight weights) is the most widely used font for Arabic and Latin bilingual signage and wayfinding around the world since 1977, for indoor and outdoor signs, airports, hospitals, and offices.

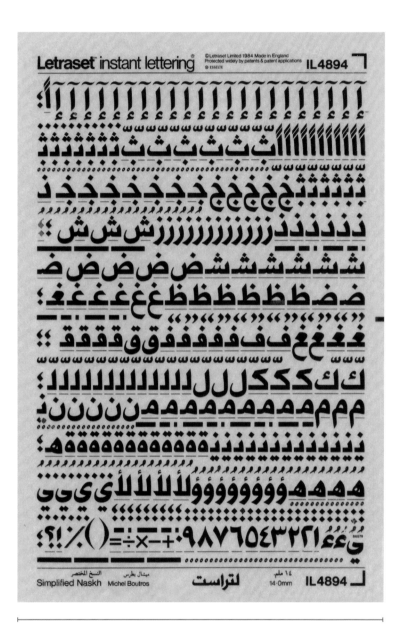

This Letraset dry-transfer lettering sheet dates back to the introduction of the Arabic line in 1976.

2•TYPE DESIGN

In 1961 Letraset Instant Lettering was introduced to the world and it was considered the most innovative typographic process since hot-metal composition. The launch and development of Letraset Instant Lettering bears comparison to the desk-top computing revolution of the late 20th century, and the digital type design and typography it permitted. In both cases, technical developments, universal availability, and a variety of typefaces created a beneficial opportunity for the user of the product. Letraset appealed to the professional graphic designer and art director, as well as the amateur publisher.

Measuring 9¾ by 15 inches, a sheet of Letraset Instant Lettering was formatted to be manageable and easily stored. Within two years, an enormous range of typefaces existed, all available in more than four sizes, with some available in ten sizes. The sheets of transfer lettering were manufactured at Letraset by silkscreen printing the letters in reverse onto one side of a polythene sheet and then overprinting the whole of the sheet with a low-tack adhesive. When the ink and adhesive dried, the sheet could be turned over and with a ball-point pen or soft-edged tool the letters were then 'rubbed down', or transferred onto paper – or any smooth surface such as glass or plastic – and, finally, using a wax-coated interleaver, the transferred letters were burnished, to remove any remaining adhesive and fix the letters firmly in position.

As a result of market demand, Letraset entered the field of Arabic typography in 1976 and went on to create more than fifty new styles, as well as a range of Arabic decorations including illuminated typefaces, Arabic sayings, borders, and ornaments. From the beginning, Letraset sought the advice and expertise of outstanding Arabic typographers and calligraphers. The result was a range of Arabic typefaces renowned for their harmony of proportion and their versatility.

Arabic Typesetting from Movable Type to the Digital Age

The first Monotype keyboard and caster modified for Arabic composition were released in 1938. A reverse delivery mechanism on the caster controlled the right to left character order. A die case with double-size matrices for deep characters like *'ain* and *jeem* and two-piece matrices for wide characters handled the extremes of character shapes. The composition keyboard, with over 200 keys, was equipped with four alphabets: separate, initial, medial, and final character forms. The typeface used was supplied from Monotype's office in India, and it had a Farsi/Urdu origin. By 1948 a more traditional Naskh from Egypt was in use and the original face was used for Farsi, Urdu, Sindhi, and Pashto. By this time further developments on the caster enabled the addition of vocalization marks and aesthetic ligatures.

The next major development was the transition from hot-metal to phototypesetter. A matrix case carrying film negatives replaced the die case; the necessity for the complex interlocking of overhanging characters and accents disappeared but the four-alphabet keyboard remained. In 1974 the 400/8 with its computer keyboard punching eight-channel tape finally replaced the four-alphabet keyboard and the thirty-one-channel tape. The phototypesetter still used a film matrix case that had grown to 400 characters, sufficient for complete, regular, and bold character sets including all accents and ligatures. Under computer control, it was also able to carry out the contextual analysis and select the correct Arabic character forms from unjustified input.

By this time three further typefaces had been developed to complement the original Monotype Urdu and Monotype Naskh faces: Solloss, a traditional Thuluth style; Mudir, a semi-bold display face of Farsi origin; and Monotype Kufi Bold, based on heavy stone carvings.

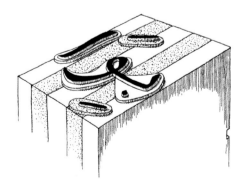

Monotype Naskh type, showing the interlocking of the vowel signs

In 1976 the Lasercomp heralded the beginning of digital typesetting. By the end of the 1970s, the existing five Arabic faces were in digital form and a new face, Akhbar, was added to provide implied character forms where in most instances the initials could also serve as medials and the separates serve as finials. Also a Moroccan face, Lakhdar Ghazal, was added. The Lasercomp enabled all seven Arabic faces to be available online together with a large number of Latin faces. It also allowed far greater control of Arabic typography; vocalization characters could be positioned accurately according to the height of the consonants and infinite numbers of aesthetic ligatures could be included. The capacity for multiple ligatures was adapted to enable the creation of a true Urdu Nastaliq typeface; ultimately 20,000 Nastaliq ligatures were digitized and a set of look-up tables located the required ligature for any given string of input characters.

The use of tens of thousands of ligatures for an Arabic typeface is a consequence of the orthodox, metal-based approach to typography. However, the fundamental difference between Latin script and Arabic script makes digitizing Arabic script more than a matter of designing a set of glyphs. DecoType was the first to tackle Arabic typography in an out-of-the-box manner, from the structure of the script, rather than ceding to the limitations of technology, and using algorithms to arrange glyphs into letter shapes. In 1985, DecoType invented the concept of the compact Dynamic Font (Smart Font, Intelligent Font), which was licensed by Microsoft ten years later in the form of an Object-linking and Embedding (OLE) server. This was to be the first smart font on any platform and proof of concept for the emerging OpenType technology.

The DecoType Advanced Composition Engine (ACE) used seventy typographic primitives (glyphlets) to cover every aspect of the Riq'a script. DecoType Nastaleeq Press today needs only 422 glyphlets to cover not just Urdu, but every Arabic-scripted language, without sacrificing *kashida* (elongating connections) or kerning. This fundamental contribution was acknowledged in 2009 with the Dr Peter Karow Award for Font Technology & Digital Typography. The work of the PKA recipients – Dr Peter Karow, digital outline fonts; DecoType, smart font technology; and Dr Donald E. Knuth, digital page layout – may be considered the pillars of modern computer typography.

DecoType's fonts in use in Brill publications. This is an example of a book by Samer Akkach, published in 2012: the body text is set in DT Naskh, with the book title in DT Nastaliq.

Unicode deals with multilingual texts. It is a new dimension of typography, the logical consequence of the internet's linking of all computers worldwide into a single communication system. Unicode is not a font, but a protocol to facilitate information interchange in all scripts of mankind. As a result, computer typography is confronted with conflicting requirements: a minimal size for speed on the web versus a large size for comprehensive language coverage and typographic precision. The litmus test for type technology today is Nastaliq or Farsi script, because of its huge number of ligatures. This is multiplied by additional characters for covering more languages, optional aesthetic variants, all of which can be stretched (*kashida*) and swashed – or both – because of its unconventional spacing requirements. Mainstream typographic technology cannot handle all these features. DecoType Nastaleeq Press, driven by ACE, is the only typeface that covers all these aspects exhaustively, without sacrificing a single Unicode language.

بہت اچھا

Wonderful

دل کہتا ہیں دنیا خرید تو مگر جیب کہتے ہے بکواس نہ کر

The heart says buy the world. But the wallet says bollocks.

خوبصورت خوبصورت کتنا حیرت انگیز کتنا حیرت انگیز کتنا حیرت انگیز شاندار شاندار افروزدگی افروزدگی ریلی ریلی سوادج سوادج تصوراتی تصوراتی بہترین بہترین غیر حقیقی حقیقی

آ آ أ إ ٱ آ آ أ إ ٱ ب ب ت ت ث ث ٹ ٹ ٹ ٹ پ پ پ پ ٹ ٹ ٹ ٹ ب ٻ ٹ ٹ ٹ ت ن ن ٮ

ج ج خ خ ح ح ٹ ٹ ج ج چ چ ڃ ڃ ڇ ڇ ڂ ڂ خ خ ح ح ڄ ڄ ٹ ٹ ح ح د د ڈ ڈ ڊ ڊ ڊ ڈ ڈ د د ڌ ڌ ذ ذ ر ر ڑ ڑ ر ر بو

ز ز ژ ژ ر ر ڑ ڑ س س ش ش ب ب پ پ ب ب ٹ ٹ ث ث ش ش س س ص ص ض ض ش ش ث ث ث ث ش ش ط ظ ظ ع ع غ غ

غ غ ع ع غ غ ع ع ف ف ف ف ب ب ف ف ٹ ٹ پ پ ق ق ۋ ۋ ی ی ٹ ٹ ق ق ف ف ٹ ٹ ک ک ک ک کئ کئ ک ک ٹ ٹ ٹ ٹ ک ک گ گ

گ گ ٹ ٹ گ گ ٹ ٹ ٹ ٹ ک ک ٹ ٹ ک ک ل ل ل ل ل ل ٹ ٹ پ پ ٹ ٹ م م ح ح م م ب ب م م ن ن ٹ ٹ ن ن ٹ ٹ ن ن ٹ ٹ

ہ ہ ۃ ۃ ھ ھ ھ ھ و و ؤ ؤ و و ۇ ۇ ۇ ۇ ۆ ۆ ۈ ۈ ۋ ۋ ۅ ۅ ی ی ئ ئ ی ی ی ی ٹ ٹ ی ی ۍ ۍ ی ی پ پ ی ی ی ی ے ے ئ ئ ے ے ے ے ئ ئ ے ے

٩ ٨ ٧ ٦ ٥ ٤ ٣ ٢ ١ ٠ ٩ ٨ ٧ ٦ ٥ ٤ ٣ ٢ ١ ٠

< = > ؛ : : / . ـ ، + ٭ ( ) ! : ؟ ٪٠٠٠ ٪٠ ٪ ٩ ٨ ٧ ٦ ٥ ٤ ٣ ٢ ١ ٠

÷ × « » { } [ ] \

بسم الله الرحمن الرحيم ريال روبية جلاله عليه السلام صلى الله عليه وسلم

10.5/22 | SHAPING & SPACING OPTIMIZED FOR ARABIC   10.5/17 | SHAPING & SPACING OPTIMIZED FOR URDU   10.5/20 | SHAPING & SPACING OPTIMIZED FOR UYGHUR

3 Logotype Design

The Value of Cultural Knowledge

While the owl symbolizes wisdom in the West, in the Middle East it is associated with death. This RasterOps campaign had to be cancelled and replaced with a totally new concept (right) created for the Middle East market. Designers cannot underestimate the importance of cultural knowledge, especially when working on projects that cross borders and languages; its role in a successful design is as integral as branding and typography.

(In the interest of visualizing an important point about the value of cultural knowledge the author has decided to use low-resolution imagery here.)

Now that a basic primer about the origins of written Arabic has been established, the issue is, how do contemporary designers best utilize Arabic for design projects?

James Joyce wrote, 'Mistakes are the portals of discovery.' He was right. Before highlighting successful combinations of Latin and Arabic typography, it is best to demonstrate the importance of being culturally versed when entering the world of multilingual or cross-cultural design, no matter what languages are being used. The table opposite features some examples that are humorous, so long as you weren't involved with these campaigns.

The Pitfalls of Not Paying Attention to Language and Culture

- The American Dairy Association was so successful with its 'Got Milk?' campaign that it was decided to extend the ads to Mexico. Unfortunately, the Spanish translation was 'Are you lactating?'

- Electrolux, a Scandinavian vacuum manufacturer, launched an advertising campaign in the United States with this catchy logo: 'Nothing sucks like an Electrolux.'

- Colgate introduced Cue toothpaste in France, but it turned out to be the same name as a well-known pornography magazine.

- When Braniff translated a slogan touting its upholstery, 'Fly in leather', it came out in Spanish as 'Fly naked'.

- American brewery Coors translated its slogan, 'Turn it loose', into Spanish: 'Suffer from diarrhea'.

- Chicken magnate Frank Perdue's motto, 'It takes a tough man to make a tender chicken', sounds much more interesting in Spanish: 'It takes a sexually stimulated man to make a chicken affectionate'.

- Clairol introduced a curling iron called the 'Mist Stick' in Germany only to find out that 'mist' is slang for manure.

- When Kentucky Fried Chicken set up shop in China, the company discovered, to their horror, that the slogan 'finger lickin' good' came out as 'eat your fingers off'.

- Parker Pens translated the slogan, 'Avoid Embarrassment – Use Quink', into Spanish: 'Evite Embarazos – Use Quink', which also means, 'Avoid Pregnancy – Use Quink'.

- In Italy, a campaign for Schweppes Tonic Water translated the name into the much less thirst-quenching 'Schweppes Toilet Water'.

- When Pepsi started marketing its products in China, they translated their slogan, 'Pepsi Brings You Back to Life'. In Chinese it reads: 'Pepsi Brings Your Ancestors Back from the Grave.'

- Chinese translation also proved difficult for Coca-Cola; it took the company two tries to get it right. They first tried 'ke-kou-ke-la' because the pronunciation sounded roughly like the name of the brand. Only after thousands of signs had been printed was it discovered that the phrase could be understood as 'bite the wax tadpole' or 'female horse stuffed with wax', depending on the dialect. The second time around, after researching 40,000 Chinese characters, Coca-Cola came up with 'ko-kou-ko-le', which translates roughly to the much more appropriate, 'happiness in the mouth'.

- The Chevy Nova never sold well in Spanish-speaking countries. 'No va' means 'it doesn't go' in Spanish.

- Ford introduced the Pinto in Brazil. After watching sales go nowhere, the company learned that 'Pinto' is Brazilian slang for 'tiny male genitals'. Ford pried the nameplates off all of the cars and substituted them with 'Corcel', which means 'steed' in Portuguese.

- When Gerber first started selling baby food in Africa, they used the same packaging as in the United States – with a cute baby on the label. Later they found out that in Africa, because many consumers cannot read, companies routinely put pictures of what's inside the packaging on the label.

- In the French-speaking part of Canada, the food company Hunt-Wesson introduced its 'Big John' products as 'Gros Jos'. It later found out that the phrase is slang for 'big breasts'.

All of these examples prove that translating a visual communication theme from one language to another is a difficult task. It is mainly advertisers and their agencies that are faced with this dilemma and cannot afford to treat the subject lightly.

In the Middle East and other Arabic-speaking countries developing campaigns and communications materials is a formidable task. Quite apart from the very real danger of offending cultural and religious sensibilities, transposing creative concepts from one language to another is always problematic and many pitfalls await the unwary. It is not simply a matter of turning a foreign language into Arabic on a word-by-word basis. Arabic copywriting skills are deeply rooted in cultural knowledge and need to be well employed in order to successfully communicate a concept or an idea coming from a different cultural background.

The following visual examples of various typographical, creative, religious, and cultural errors clearly illustrate some of the hazards when considering the use of Arabic, and demonstrate just how easily costly mistakes can be made and creative concepts destroyed when designers attempt to use Arabic without the necessary knowledge.

In 2011 the so-called 'Arab Spring' dominated the news. The world watched as citizens clashed with and overthrew long-standing power structures across the Middle East and North Africa. The struggle between rebels and Muammar Gaddafi supporters in Libya resulted in a hotly debated international intervention. But even with the eyes of the world on this North African nation, CNN made the unfortunate mistake of confusing Tripoli, Lebanon, with Tripoli, Libya. This very blatant fact-checking error implies an assumption about cultures that is unacceptable in the 21st century.

(In the interest of visualizing an important point about the value of cultural knowledge the author has decided to use low-resolution imagery here.)

All languages contain idiomatic words and expressions that are impossible to translate literally, if at all. When considering launching a product or campaign in a new market where a different language is spoken, it is imperative to use local knowledge in order to avoid unintentional puns and gaffes. For example, it would not be advisable to launch this Nestle product in Arabic-speaking markets because 'air' refers to the penis.

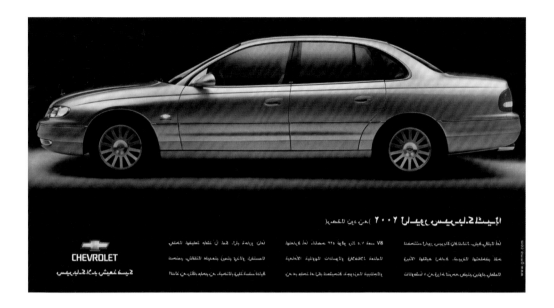

This Chevrolet ad in Arabic looks good so long as you don't try to read it. The text is printed so it reads like a mirror image of how it should read; everything is inverted – no doubt a costly mistake for the company.

Virgin Atlantic placed an advertisement in *The Mail on Sunday* on Sunday 5 February 2006 announcing its Dubai route, starting from 27 March 2006. Running a full-colour page spread, it read 'shortly' in Arabic, pronounced *kariban*. By not using the accents above the final letter *aleph*, the pronunciation is *kariba*. So a grammatical mistake was made.

Two days later, on 7 February 2006, another Virgin Atlantic advertisement appeared in the *Evening Standard*. It was the same publishing house, announcing the same Dubai route, yet they bizarrely changed the character design of *qaf* to a *ha* with two dots above, creating an unknown character in the Arabic language.

Below, the word 'shortly' set in Arabic shows the real shapes of the characters making the word perfectly legible.

قريبًا

It is advisable for all visual communication in Arabic-speaking countries to acknowledge the tenets of Islam, the same as non-Muslim Arabic speakers do wherever they might live. Real Madrid removed the cross from their official logo out of respect for Muslim supporters in the United Arab Emirates (UAE).

Here is an example of one of the more common errors made by non-Arabic speakers adapting ad campaigns for Arab markets. The designers did not take into consideration the fact that Arabic reads from right to left. In this example, the headline says: From a dish that goes far back in the past, we developed advanced dishes to receive the latest signals in technology.

Reading from left to right the concept is fine. The way the advertisement was run, however, inverted the message, suggesting that the company went from satellite dishes back to ceramic bowls.

(*In the interest of visualizing an important point about the value of cultural knowledge the author has decided to use low-resolution imagery here, reproduced directly from a newspaper.*)

The Highs and Lows of Logotype Conversion

When considering what elements of design to utilize when working with Arabic and other languages, it is important not to fall into the comparison trap. As static as the self-imposed isolation made it, Arabic typography has a life of its own. In the 21st century, however, it needs to be re-evaluated. While it is important to consider the similarities and differences between Arabic and Latin typography, it is dangerous to dwell too long on comparing the two. This is simply another kind of stagnation that will not result in progress.

It is important to understand what the West did when they developed their own typefaces during the Industrial Revolution and try to apply it to Arabic design and typography. New typefaces need to have an identity that reflects the cultures of Arabic-speaking populations. Latin and Arabic typographies should interact as if putting two cultures together. Once each one shows its own identity in the design of the artwork, the typographies will work concurrently. Modifying the combination of both typographies will allow the viewer to feel more engaged.

Designed by Dave Farey, Richard Dawson, and Arlette and Mourad Boutros, Tanseek was the 21st century's first multilingual range of typefaces. This harmonious range of Arabic-Latin (serif and sans serif) typefaces serves the needs of today's international creative industries. It is an efficient and adaptable match with the most commonly used Latin fonts.

One of the greatest challenges for designers and calligraphers is producing Arabic conversions of established logotypes that are perfectly balanced for style, weight, and legibility. More than just fashionable, the demands of the international marketplace demand regularly converting logotypes from Latin into Arabic and vice versa. Of course, there are numerous factors to consider when undertaking a design project that requires a logotype conversion or multilingual signage.

Advertisers translating their messages into Arabic often ask whether Arabic is one language or several. Differences in dialects in Arabic-speaking countries, and between regions, do exist, but in terms of the written word, Arabic can be regarded as one script, known as Classical Arabic or Fouss'ha. The following examples touch on some of the more important issues that need to be kept in mind as they account for some of these differences.

Example of Tanseek Modern in use on TV

When tooth-shaped characters such as *ba* and *noon* are followed by *ya*, they turn into an inverted shape from which the following letter hangs. This is an age-old tradition used in all rounded scripts. There are numerous prominent companies throughout the Middle East with the letters *noon* and *ya* as in *al watani* (which means 'the national'), or *ba* and *ya* as in 'Dubai', at the end of their names. It is interesting to note the different treatments it receives. A common mistake is to use the inverted shape when there is no need for it, especially in the word 'Dubai' as shown below. Some fonts have the final *ya* with the additional shape, which usually refers to another letter, mistakenly treating it as part of the letter *ya*. In the *al watani* example below, the correct writing uses the inverted shape to denote the letter *noon*. If the standard tooth shape of *noon* is to be used, then keeping the inverted shape is an erroneous duplication.

inverted tooth shape   standard tooth shape

When *noon*, and other tooth-shaped characters, is followed by *ya* it becomes an inverted tooth as shown on the first line. The latter shape is often mistakenly seen to be part of final *ya* as shown in the word *al watani* on the second line.

This confusion happens also in the word 'Dubai' for example. The final *ya* shouldn't have the inverted tooth when it connects to the letter *ba*, which sits under it.

While doing transliterations, many English phonetics do not have alphabetical equivalents in Arabic. For this reason, it has become common to use the nearest letter to transliterate Latin alphabet phonetics. One example is the letter *jeem*. In most Arabic-speaking countries, it is pronounced like the 'j' in 'bonjour' or like the 'dg' in 'budget'; but in Egypt this letter is pronounced like the 'g' in 'guess'.

Consider the shapes of Latin letters and compare them to Arabic shapes; there are many similarities. For example, take the letter 'm' and flip it upside down and it becomes the first segment of the letter *seen* in Arabic. It is worth noting that using the shapes of Latin letters and numerals to convey meaning was widely used as mobile phones and text messaging became a standard means of communication. Before an Arabic interface was created for mobile phones, Arabic-speaking users had to send text messages using the Latin alphabet to express Arabic words; this was most commonly achieved by inserting numbers (that is, Arabic numerals 0 to 9) between Latin alphabet letters. Even after mobile phones were equipped with an Arabic interface, users continued to use this typographic hybrid out of habit.

Through many variations of tilting, twisting, rotating, and mirroring Latin letters, Arabic letterforms can be created. The danger in such an exercise, however, is that the callow logotype converter risks creating a form that no matter how visually arresting, is culturally insensitive. Conversely, the advantage of such tinkering is that it is easy to conserve the text weight, serifs, x-height, and stems of individual letters, though even these factors often skew proportions and serious adjustments to the letterforms are required.

Al Danah Mouassal is a tobacco that comes in a variety of flavours. What these images demonstrate is the importance of understanding how various Arabic-speaking countries translate Arabic differently. In Egypt the word for 'strawberry' is pronounced *farawla*, while in Lebanon it is pronounced *fraise*. In the example on the right, the image of a peach is for the Lebanese market, but for the Saudi market it is a plum. In an Arabic dictionary the definition of the Arabic word for 'peach' is both 'peach' and 'plum', while the definition for 'plum' is simply 'plum'. Such aspects of the language make it critical for companies creating advertising campaigns to understand these important differences.

All of this stems from an understanding of Arabic calligraphy and typography. Before blazing ahead into the future, we need to return to the roots of the written language in order to design for today and create materials required by the global marketplace.

On the following pages Arabic logotypes of international brands nearly mirror the original Latin logotypes and splendidly demonstrate the calligrapher's art.

Successful Logos

Radius

The international computer hardware manufacturer executed a conversion of Latin into Arabic that possesses the same block feeling of the original Latin logo with one ascender, the *aleph* visually balancing the lowercase 'd'. Another strong aspect of the conversion is the red 'i' in the Latin version where the Arabic letter *ya* becomes the visual equivalent. Note that *ya* does not have the same shape of the 'i', yet it works perfectly because the conversion respects Arabic typography and the years of culture that it carries. As a result, the design maintains legibility, style, and balance.

Tarbouche

Here is an example of a logotype conversion from Arabic to Latin. The traditional Mediterranean fast food restaurant that started in Abu Dhabi wanted to open international franchises. The Arabic logotype was done by hand tracing the two words on top of one another, rendering an image that can only be considered as personal calligraphy. Arabic calligraphy was used to produce the Latin version of this logo. The designer did not forget that Latin text also has its own rules and regulations. These were followed, with a twist, in order to create an equivalent to the Arabic logo.

Rainbow – Abou Kaouss

When the initial market survey was conducted, it was discovered that transliterating the Rainbow Quality Milk logo into the exact pronunciation of 'rainbow' would not be helpful because the consumers, inspired by the rainbow visual on the package, were calling it *abou kaouss*. It was decided that 'Abou Kaouss' would be the name for the Arabic corporate identity. This didn't harm the brand at all. On the contrary, it gave the consumers security because it suggested that the makers of the product understood their needs and culture. The logo shows the clean-cut typography and the respect of the Arabic rules of designing a typeface. Visually, the two logos work perfectly together. The subtlety of Arabic details gives the Arabic logo the extra dimension necessary when converting Latin into Arabic.

Jebel Ali

When developing brand identities for the Middle East and adding Arabic elements to any logo, it was common to use an Arabic or Islamic pattern reference and adapt visuals from those patterns. Unfortunately, most of the time it created more of a religious look. In the case of the Oasis Beach Hotel and the Jebel Ali Hotel and Golf Resort owned by Jebel Ali International Hotel Group (UAE), the designers borrowed the concept directly from the Arabic calligraphy. The outcome confirmed that bamboo calligraphy can be creatively used in order to create visual signifiers. Both the seahorse and the peacock have the aspects of Arabic calligraphy enriched by rhombic dots but actually cannot be read. It is simply an abstraction using a cultural technique representing a unique visual to achieve the required aims.

Oasis Beach Hotel

Jebel Ali Hotel & Golf Resort

بنك قطر الأول

QFB

The logo was created for Qatar First Bank, with Arabic calligraphy at its core due to its cultural significance, versatility, and beauty. The word 'first' in Arabic is created in Diwani style to emulate the Latin letter 'Q', for Qatar.

The conversion of the logos for the British soft drink company Britvic from Latin typography to Arabic typography showcases the obvious and the subtle elements of logotype conversions. Clearly, the colours remain the same, as do the lines around the text. Notice, however, the shift in orientation of the logos for the orange and lemon flavours. This was done to compensate for the fact that the two languages read in opposite directions.

drive communication
Member of the **dentsu** Network

'Drive Communication' is a good example that shows the flexibility of Arabic and the ability of its calligraphic nature to blend into multiple cultures and languages.

A Series of Logos for the Group of HH Sheikh Mansoor Bin Zayed Al Nahyan, UAE

مهرجان سُمُّو الشيخ منصور بن زايد آل نهيان
العالمي للخيول العربية الأصيلة

HH Sheikh Mansoor Bin Zayed Al Nahyan
Global Arabian Horse Flat Racing Festival

تاج جوهرة الشيخ زايد بن سلطان آل نهيان
Sheikh Zayed Bin Sultan Al Nahyan Jewel Crown

وثبة ستاليونز
Wathba Stallions

كأس
الشيخ محمد بن منصور
بن زايد آل نهيان
لسباقات القدرة

SHEIKH MOHAMMED BIN MANSOOR
BIN ZAYED AL NAHYAN
ENDURANCE CUP

بطولة سمو الشيخة
فاطمة بنت مبارك لسيدات القدرة
H.H. Sheikha Fatima Bint Mubarak Ladies
Endurance CEIO Championship

4 Case Studies

The Essence of Newspaper Design:
The Times of London

Dave Farey

'Waves of technological change over the past 25 years have rewritten the rules of what is possible in the design of a paper and the way it happens.'
– Simon Esterson on contemporary newspaper design

Some forty-five years ago, Harold Evans and Allen Hutt, men with vast experience of graphic design and journalism, pioneered a new understanding of newspaper layout and typography. 'A proper marriage between graphic design and journalism can produce a new dimension of communication – provided that mutual respect for the rules binding each partner's contribution is observed', wrote Harold Evans, in his introduction to *Newspaper Graphics* in 1970. And Allen Hutt wrote for the *Monotype Recorder* that 'the aim of this departure from the tradition of grey pillars is fundamentally to make the newspaper more inviting and more easily legible to the casual reader'.

The major constraints for achieving this synergy are the same as they have always been in the newspaper business, at least up until recently. First, a resistance to change by owners, publishers, and editors, as their wish would be to maintain a conformity of visual presentation that was traditionally acceptable to their readers. Secondly, and an invisible element to the readers, was the continuous and relentless march of technology for the improvement of newspaper production and to maximize economy, both financially and for work efficiency.

In 1970 Allen Hutt wrote, 'Times Roman, in short, was designed for production conditions which have ceased to exist'. He was describing the changing circumstances of print production and quality of paper. In 1932, the year of the introduction of the typeface Times Roman, *The Times* of London had a single nightly print run of less than 60,000 copies, printed on high-quality absorbent paper. By 1970 the print run had increased

How *The Times* used to look

THE TIMES

Max 24C min 6C   Wednesday August 31 2016 | thetimes.co.uk | No 72003   Only 80p to subscribers £1.40

Secrets of the Vogue girls
Inside the fashion bible

INSIDE TIMES2

Carol Midgley
Jilly Cooper,
posh men & sex

Signal from the stars could be ET phoning planet Earth

Oliver Moody Science Correspondent

Was it a bird? Was it a plane? Or was it a 95-year-old Mayday message from an alien radio ham?

A flash of microwave radiation registered on a Russian telescope has become the new focus of the hunt for intelligent life outside our solar system.

The violent burst, which lasted about two seconds on May 15 last year, appeared to have come from a star in the Hercules constellation.

The Search for Extraterrestrial Intelligence (Seti) institute is to turn its most powerful telescopes on HD 164595, a star similar to the Sun but nearly 100 light years from the Earth. So far it has found nothing untoward.

Seth Shostak, a senior astronomer at the organisation, said that it would take an alien civilisation as much energy as all of humanity generates to create a beacon bright enough to generate the Hercules flash. He said that the team would carry on looking, but accused Russia of breaching protocol by failing to alert other researchers while there was time to confirm the observation.

Scientists in Paris are checking whether the signal could have been bent out of line by the star's gravity. Researchers have found only one planet orbiting HD 164595, a gassy, Neptune-like world that is unlikely to be capable of supporting life.

Lord Rees of Ludlow, the Astronomer Royal, said that the blip on the Russian telescope was worth studying but was not proof of alien civilisation.

Alan Penny, honorary reader in astronomy at the University of St Andrews and organiser of the UK Seti Research Network, pointed out that the reading could have been caused by anything from a stray TV transmission to agricultural equipment or a well-concealed spy satellite.

Aliens calling, page 11
Leading article, page 25

Corbyn on course to win bigger mandate

Rival's supporters ready to split, Times poll finds

Francis Elliott Political Editor

Jeremy Corbyn is on course to win the Labour leadership contest with an increased mandate thanks to overwhelming backing from the party's newest supporters.

Mr Corbyn is leading his rival, Owen Smith, by 62 per cent to 38 per cent, according to the first published poll of those entitled to vote in the election. Last year Mr Corbyn secured a 59 per cent share of the vote.

The results of the YouGov survey for *The Times* suggest that the summer coup by Labour MPs against their leader is likely to fail, and that the party might split. Voting in the contest opened last week and the winner will be announced on September 24, the eve of the Labour Party conference.

The poll will embolden Corbyn supporters calling for a purge of critical MPs, with 48 per cent of eligible voters in favour of forcing all sitting members to face constituency ballots before being allowed to stand again.

The poll shows that Mr Smith has failed to make inroads with Corbynistas even after adopting a series of left-wing policies and despite months of bitter attacks on the leader from prominent figures across the party.

Mr Corbyn is being heavily backed by registered supporters and newer members as well as most union affiliates, the poll suggests. The strength of that backing outweighs low support among longstanding party members. Some 640,500 people are eligible to vote in the Labour contest. More than half are full members who joined the party last year or earlier.

Among those who became members before May last year, support for Mr Smith is high, at 68 per cent compared with 32 per cent for Mr Corbyn, according to the YouGov poll. It drops to 28 per cent for Mr Smith for those who joined between May and September, and to 14 per cent for those who signed up after September, underlining Mr Corbyn's popularity among newer members.

A further 129,000 paid a one-off £25 fee to become registered supporters before January this year. The challenger's hopes of unseating Mr Corbyn rest on winning over this group. However, Mr Smith is attracting only one in four, with 70 per cent opting for Mr Corbyn and the remainder undecided.

The remaining 168,000 voters are union affiliates, and Mr Corbyn is in the lead among this group, on 54 per cent against Mr Smith's 33 per cent.

The poll shows that Mr Corbyn would be heading for an even more convincing victory if his opponents had not won a court action that barred new Labour members from voting. The Court of Appeal ruled this month that Labour's national executive committee had the right to bar 130,000 members who had signed up since January.

Amid growing animosity between

Continued on page 2, col 3

Art of spin Ed Balls takes to the floor with Laura Whitmore, a fellow contestant on Strictly Come Dancing, at its red carpet launch. The BBC show starts on Saturday

Patients ten times more likely to die in cancer lottery

Katie Gibbons

Cancer patients are ten times more likely to die within a month of starting chemotherapy at some hospitals than others, an NHS study has found.

"Over-enthusiastic" prescribing of chemotherapy drugs, which damage the immune system, and a failure to monitor patients at home for signs of deadly infections may contribute to higher mortality rates, experts said.

Public Health England has told 19 hospital trusts to review their cancer treatment "as a matter of urgency" after the new data showed that too many patients died within 30 days.

The study of more than 30,000 patients with breast or lung cancer, published today in *The Lancet Oncology*, is the first to collect chemotherapy mortality data of this kind at a national level. The authors, who surveyed 147 trusts, acknowledge that small patient samples and poor data management may have contributed to some results. However, the findings will raise fears of a postcode lottery in cancer care.

The number of cancer patients given chemotherapy has risen sharply in the past 30 years. The treatment, in which cancer cells are attacked with intravenous drugs or tablets, is used alone or with radiotherapy and other drugs.

About 55,000 women in Britain are found to have breast cancer each year; 40 per cent receive chemotherapy. It is the first course of treatment for most people with small cell lung cancer, which accounts for about 12 per cent of diagnoses each year. The average death rate for such patients was 2.9 per cent, rising to 10 per cent for those whose lung cancer was terminal.

At Royal Bournemouth and Christchurch hospitals, 26 per cent of lung cancer patients who had chemotherapy died within 30 days of starting treatment. This compared with an effective mortality risk of 0 per cent at nearby Taunton and Somerset hospitals, the study found.

For breast cancer patients the risk of

Continued on page 6, col 4

The current look of the paper.

to over 400,000, across four editions. The technology of printing had changed radically from hot-metal setting to offset rotary printing over forty years, and the amount of ink deposited on paper was less than before. Consequently, the typeface Times Roman did not perform as well with these changes. To accommodate this, in 1972 a new text typeface, Times Europa designed by Walter Tracy, was introduced to improve legibility for the increased demands of production at *The Times*.

This was a technology-driven typographic change – not a design change. However, six years before in 1966, *The Times* had taken the design decision of showing 'news' on the front page, whereas from 1788 until 1966 it had been dominated by a mixture of theatre announcements and single-column advertisements for every conceivable item, from cough medicines to Rolls-Royce cars.

In 1981 Times Roman returned as the text typeface for *The Times* when technology once more dictated the design pace with the introduction of phototypesetting production. But by 1990 this system had been overtaken by computer-driven typesetting. In 1991 Times Millennium was commissioned and that typeface lasted for eleven years until 2002, when the newspaper decided to address the problem of the deficiency of black ink on paper, caused by the introduction of full-colour printing during the 1990s. Typographically, the result was Times Classic, a family of text and display typefaces that were more robust and denser than previous typefaces and could be used across a variety of supplements and paper stock.

Both Evans's and Hutt's best intentions have been realized in the 21st century, in *The Times* and most news-driven daily newspapers. This has been due to a combination of the developments in computer and digital technologies, and the consequent understanding by design directors, designers, and editors of the advantages that these processes have created. All journalists and sub-editors are on board with design technology, which is a remarkable turn of events, but completely understandable given today's methods of creating a newspaper. Technology has allowed journalists to enter their copy directly onto a page, to view not only their article but the whole of the page and the whole construction of the newspaper. Obviously, the process must be coordinated efficiently by sub-editors and planned by production staff, but a complex process can be simplified in essence from an article being written and placed in position, and to be as quick as it takes to perform those tasks.

The Times paper format in 2002 was described as 'broadsheet', that is 58 x 37 cm with a centre horizontal fold, as were all its competitors in the British 'quality' market. This format allowed for flexibility within page formats, in particular, for four or five major stories plus photos on the front page, and when necessary for content information as a colour band to appear above, or in some cases, below the masthead. The broadsheet format consisted on average of forty pages, with eight columns to a page, broken into one to six columns for each story with headings either in single or double lines, occasionally more, to suit the page layout.

Newspaper sizes during the early years of the 21st century in Britain became the latest battleground for readership, influenced in the main for stabilizing or increasing sales, potentially with younger generations of readers. Traditionally 'quality' papers have tried to anticipate older generations changing reading habits and their willingness to read different papers because of targeted promotions or important stories. Inevitably, with increased competition from other communication providers, such as TV and the internet, newspaper readership has been difficult to maintain, let alone increase. Equally, newspapers are very conscious of the influence and purchasing power of both genders, and in particular that professional women account for a large percentage of their current or potential readers, and this needs to be reflected on the page.

As it happens, *The Times* had been planning to change its format since 2002, following research that indicated a smaller, 'friendlier' size would be favoured – for a variety of reasons – by younger readers. This radical step, to produce a tabloid that is half the physical size of a broadsheet, or a 'compact' as *The Times* refers to it, required a complete re-evaluation, editorially as well as graphically. As often happens in launch situations, *The Times* were preempted by *The Independent* newspaper by three months in its switch to compact; *The Independent* changed format in September 2003, and *The Times* in December 2003. *The Times* continued to run the broadsheet and compact versions side by side until November 2004, and then permanently dropped the larger format that had existed in varying broadsheet sizes since 1788. Sizes had increased since that date from 47 x 32 cm to 62 x 47 cm by the early 20th century, and had declined by increments during the following hundred years, to the modern broadsheet in 2002.

NEWSPAPER OF THE YEAR

THE TIMES

Max 10C min -8C

Thursday March 3 2016 | thetimes.co.uk | No 71848

Only 80p to print members £1.20

INSIDE TIMES2

Is it time to stop tipping?
The great gratuity debate

Let's speak out over failed welfare state

Jenni Russell, Opinion, page 25

£100m bill for licence fee dodgers after BBC closes loophole

Elizabeth Rigby Media Editor
Frances Gibb Legal Editor

More than a million people who exploit a loophole to watch the BBC without a television licence will be forced to pay up within months under new laws.

Households watching programmes on iPlayer after they have aired on television do not currently have to pay

the £145.50 fee — a situation that is forecast to cost the BBC £100 million a year.

The culture secretary announced yesterday that he would rush through legislation to close the loophole and make non-payment a criminal offence as early as the summer.

"The BBC works on the basis that all who watch it pay for it," John Whitting-

dale told the Oxford Media Convention. "Giving a free ride to those who enjoy Sherlock or Bake Off an hour, a day or a week after they are broadcast was never intended and is wrong."

Launched in 2007 the iPlayer pioneered online streaming for a mass audience but has become a bugbear for the corporation as growing numbers of households dodge the licence fee by

watching programmes after they are first aired. The BBC said that the loophole would cost it £100 million a year in lost revenues by 2022, equivalent to nearly 700,000 households not paying the fee.

The corporation is considering how to enforce the new rules. Options include asking viewers to sign in to iPlayer — perhaps with a unique user

code — and monitoring whether households have a TV licence when they access the catch-up service. The BBC said that it had not yet worked through the details of enforcement and that there were a number of "complex factors" to consider.

It was too early to say whether the new regime would allow members of

Continued on page 2, col 3

BEN LACK

Adam Johnson leaves court after being convicted of sexual activity with a 15-year-old fan. He was warned to expect jail and told to "say goodbye" to his daughter

Club allowed paedophile footballer to keep playing

Katie Gibbons

Sunderland football club allowed Adam Johnson to play on for months — earning about £3 million — despite having details of child sex charges against him.

The club was facing questions after Johnson, 28, was found guilty of sexually touching a 15-year-old fan. He is the first Premier League and England player to face jail for such a crime.

The £10 million winger was suspended after his arrest in March last year but returned to the pitch within weeks.

During the trial it emerged that Johnson and his lawyers met Margaret Byrne, Sunderland's chief executive, on May 4 and told her "everything" about his contact with the girl.

On the understanding that he would deny the charges, Johnson was allowed to play another 28 times. His final game was on February 6, days before he changed his plea to admit two of the four charges. The club said that had it known he intended to plead guilty it would have terminated his contract immediately.

Footballer faces five years in jail, page 7
He betrayed club he loved, pages 66-67

Putin 'weaponising' migrants

● Russian president wants Europe overwhelmed, Nato warns ● Britain and France develop new round of military drones

David Charter Berlin
Andrew Rettman Brussels
Michael Savage
Chief Political Correspondent

Nato has accused President Putin of weaponising the migrant crisis in an effort to push Europe to the brink of collapse.

As Britain was told to pay £63 million to help Greece to cope with soaring numbers of trapped incomers, Russia and Syria were blamed for intensifying the tension between allies.

"Together, Russia and the Assad re-

gime are deliberately weaponising migration in an attempt to overwhelm European structures and break European resolve," General Philip Breedlove, Nato's top commander in Europe, said.

Russia's actions in Syria "wildly exacerbated the problem", he told a Senate committee in Washington. The Syrian regime's use of barrel bombs against civilians was terrorising people to "get them on the road" and make them a problem for other countries.

While those fleeing Syria's civil war and Islamic State were legitimate refugees, General Breedlove said that

there had been a change in recent months. "This criminality, the terrorists and the returning foreign fighters are clearly a daily part of the refugee flow in Europe," he said.

David Cameron will unveil a £1.5 billion deal with the French government today to develop the next generation of drones amid the growing threat of Middle East instability engulfing the West.

Speaking before a UK-France summit in Amiens, the prime minister said that the two nations were "proud allies" that worked together to improve security. His words will prompt claims that

the deal is in part designed to maintain good relations in the run-up to the EU referendum.

The refugee issue caused tempers to flare between EU leaders yesterday, with the Austrian chancellor defending its cap on migrants by declaring that "Austria is not a waiting room for Germany" and attacking Angela Merkel for her "chaotic" approach to asylum seekers.

More than 2,000 people a day are crossing the Aegean to Greece and trying to get to the West, causing an increasingly volatile bottleneck of up to

15,000 migrants on its northern border, where Macedonia has now restricted entrants to 250 a day.

Efforts were also under way to convince Turkey to take part in a German-led scheme to retain the 2.5 million Syrians on its territory before an EU summit on Monday.

The pressures facing Greece led the European Commission to propose a new fund of €700 million over three years including €82.6 million from Britain, with up to €300 million available this year. It will come from money that
Continued on page 2, col 3

The digital edition of the paper

During the period when two issues of *The Times*, broadsheet and compact, were published on the same day – essentially to allow the readers to get used to the change – it gave an invaluable opportunity to the editorial staff and the designers to improve and distil the compact format. A forty-page paper developed into eighty pages as a compact, and the columns reduced from eight to six, with a slightly wider measure. The text sizes and leading remained the same, but the headlines were kept short where practical and headlines were no larger than 54 point to allow as much freedom as possible for photos and illustrations.

Whereas the front cover of *The Times* as a broadsheet would carry an average of four stories, the compact version would be restricted to one or two. The cover also featured one column, normally on the left, to introduce stories in the main paper – but not as an index – which was placed deliberately across two columns on page two, giving a full synopsis page by page under section heads. The aim of the compact version was to create 'verticality' or, to use the opened double page in a vertical manner. As a general rule stories would not run horizontally across two pages and, where possible and practical, pages reflected each other left to right, and this was encouraged by the positioning of advertising space. Where a story was complex or sufficiently long, 'pull quotes' – larger text set in a single column featuring an important element of the story – were positioned for maximum effect. And carefully positioned throughout the paper were single-column announcements on a tonal background, outlining specific stories in other sections, and providing navigational aids to encourage the reader to use the paper to the best advantage.

Ultimately, there are two tests for the success of a redesign, or in the case of the compact *Times*, it was more of a relaunch, or to some extent a new paper. First, to make the 'navigation' work in such a way that regular items, such as foreign news, business, sports, obituaries, the letters page, weather maps, and the crossword, were regularly placed day by day so that readers were reassured and familiar with the content. Secondly, to gauge the success of the relaunch by sales performance. Fifteen months into *The Times* compact format, the audited sales figures showed an annual increase of 6.6 per cent, with all other comparable British quality papers losing sales from between

1 per cent and 7 per cent. Of course, it cannot be claimed that a redesign alone would create the added sales; in this case, it is a peculiar combination of a redesign being dictated by a format change, based on a judgment about the aspirations and inclinations of their readers. Even so, during the same period, *The Independent*, which had switched to a compact format, lost 1 per cent of their sales and the three other quality papers lost an average of 5 per cent.

So the decision to switch *The Times* size and format from broadsheet to compact, or tabloid, proved an initial success. But in 2005 Neville Brody, the highly regarded editorial designer – among his other accomplishments – was asked to take a fresh look at *The Times* design and format. One significant advance after the period of conversion of *The Times* from broadsheet to compact was the technological ability of the newspaper presses to print colour on both sides, whereas previously a left-hand side could have been black only, facing a right-hand side of full colour or vice versa.

Brody explained that he judged the format to be stale, and 'with *The Times* downsizing from a mansion to a semi detached, they didn't throw anything out, and it was my job to help them declutter'. So for visual rebalance, the process 'became story led not design led, as we've tried to bring articulation between news copy and opinion pieces'. To this end, Brody decided the compact format needed a more condensed Roman headline family, which he and his team at Research Studios in London completed and launched with the redesigned newspaper in November 2006.

Brody's new family of fonts is called Times Modern and used as headlines for news stories, contrasting with the sans serif font Gotham for section headings, opinion pieces, and non-news articles. The family of Times Modern has been extended since 2006 by Art Editors Jon Hill and Matt Brown, with additional weights primarily for the sophisticated magazine sections and the Saturday change of editorial pace. Six new fonts were designed as companions to Times Modern, but with an eye on the growing and absolute necessity to develop the typographic style of *The Times* for non-print media and readers' consumption of non-print media through websites, tablets, and smartphones.

The Times has been online since 1999. But time and technology have moved along. With the switch from ink to pixel, the improvement in screen resolution, and the migration of readers to digital, according to *The Times* digital design editor, Nicola Ryan, *The Times* has moved 'away from designing one product – the paper – towards designing multiple experiences, websites, tablet apps, smartphones, podcasts. These have their own challenges and demand individual design approaches. The growing number of people reading news on screens will mean that news design must become increasingly interactive, with animation, sound, and video playing a big part in our daily news consumption.'

To maintain readership awareness and quality of all typographic elements, *The Times* iPad uses its real fonts rather than JPEG or PDF substitute images for its page construction, the text remaining sharp when turned from vertical to horizontal. Accordingly, the relationship of the printed and digital versions of *The Times*'s news output is enhanced by the use of the same fonts. In 2016 the technical challenge of completing the circle for its website was fulfilled when the exclusive Times Digital fonts were put in place, which for visual and technical reasons are heavier in weight than the newspaper text font, Times Classic. The new digital fonts are a design combination of Times Classic and Times Modern, ensuring clarity and continuity across the newspaper and the website.

The Times, along with all other printed papers, magazines, and journals, has faced and will continue to face, the ever increasing demands of the changing world and competition from all of the media outlets that provide global news, opinion, features, and titillation. Thankfully, *The Times* has proved more than once in its long history that it is adaptable. As a previous editor stated at the turn of the millennium: '[A]lthough the coming revolution in information technology is a potential threat to newspapers, it is also a great opportunity.'

Al Hayat

First printed in Beirut in 1946, *Al Hayat*, meaning 'life' in Arabic, now prints, in different editions, its daily paper in Beirut, Cairo, Dubai, Dammam, Jeddah, Riyadh, Frankfurt, and London. In 2004 *Al Hayat* decided to assess its visual identity, take stock of its visual appeal, and create a new style that would relate to its existing readership yet reach out to a younger market.

Al Hayat, issue No. 1

There were three reasons for a redesign: first, to increase the presence of *Al Hayat* in the Arab-speaking markets; secondly to take into account rival newspapers; thirdly to balance that with first attracting and then keeping new readers. In this regard, *Al Hayat* is similar to all national and international daily papers, with the exception that it is also published for readers in Europe. Readers of *Al Hayat* in Europe have access to Western

Old layout design

AL HAYAT
الحياة
www.alhayat.com
على iPad
و iPhone
و Android؟
هل جربت قراءة
إمت الحياة عقيدة وجهاد
الحياة كيف كنت تتجاوبا على جميع التطبيقات
٣٠ صفحة
السبت ٢ نيسان (أبريل) ٢٠١٦ الموافق ٢٤ جمادى الثانية ١٤٣٧ هـ، العدد ١٩٣٥٦
ALHAYAT SATURDAY 2 APRIL 2016 ISSUE NO 19356

خبراء دوليون في الرياض وصنعاء لتحضير محادثات الكويت

ولي ولي العهد قال لـ"بلومبيرغ" إن "أرامكو" ستحول الى تكتل صناعي
تريليونا دولار لصندوق سيادي سعودي

(التتمة ص ٥)

تبادل اتهامات بسبب تقرير "الحياة" ... وبوتين قلق من طلب الرئيس السوري الدعم الإيراني
واشنطن تتمسك بـ"تنحي الأسد في مرحلة انتقالية"

بوتين مستقبلاً الحريري في الكرملين (أ.س.أ.ف)

العربية تغلق مكاتبها... واستهداف مكتب الشرق الأوسط في بيروت

الحريري يلمس إصرار بوتين على "الحل الدولي" في سورية

جنود قرب مدينة تدمر (أ.ف.ب)

أشاد بنجاح خطوات تطبيق الاتفاق مع إيران
أوباما يؤكد تدارك "القنبلة القذرة" لـ"داعش"

الأكراد يرفضون التشكيلة الحكومية وأطراف أخرى تستعد لمعارضتها
عوائق دستورية وسياسية تواجه العبادي

(التتمة ص ٦)

تنامي موجة التأييد لحكومة الوفاق الليبية... والفويل يتراجع
السراج يصلي الجمعة في وسط طرابلس

لبنيون يستقبلون فايز السراج في طرابلس (أ.ف.ب)

New layout design

newspapers – although obviously in a different language with different editorial views and emphasis. But these European readers would take note of the stylistic changes in the paper's layout. The design style was editorially led. The paper's tendency to put as many news articles on the front page as would fit often resulted in as many as twelve stories competing for attention. Invariably, all the articles started on the front page continued inside, but with no real flow on the continuation page. Although standard for the readers of *Al Hayat* through force of habit, it was disturbing to the rhythm of reading the paper – the need to flip back and forth repeatedly derailed any focus or emphasis that major or minor news stories might have.

Other pan-Arab newspapers had fewer stories on the front pages, between six and eight. The average number of stories carried on British, European, and American front pages is five. *Al Hayat* aimed for this, not simply to relate visually to international papers, but because it made sense for the readers' appreciation of the news.

In general, the internal pages of *Al Hayat*, before the redesign, were better formatted than the front page, although there was an inconsistency of style and use of horizontal and vertical rules from page to page. Typographically, in terms of balance and emphasis for headlines, *Al Hayat* used one weight of font in two sizes as a headline and a subhead, and the subhead was often above the headline. These visually competed for attention and a lighter weight of subhead would have been just as efficient in the context of the articles and the overall appearance of the page. The visual appearance as a whole would benefit if all articles were treated in this way. The consistent use of horizontal rules would also improve the structure of the page and be more harmonious than before.

The text font was very heavy, a slightly lighter weight would appear more comfortable and would have a better overall balance. Ranging the headlines to the right would also improve the structure of page. The use of an 'inside contents' column on the front page was very useful. It informed the reader of other items that would no longer appear on the front page, creating interest and helping the reader navigate through the newspaper by flagging regular columns and features. It also added colour and a strong design element to the identity and structure of the page.

محمد عبده وأثره الفكري والتربوي على ما روى طه حسين في كتاب «الأيام»

■ مصطفى الجوزو *

مجمع الفقه الإسلامي الدولي وسبل مواجهته التحديات الحضارية المعاصرة

■ حسن سفر *

الحياة

www.alhayat.com

ALHAYAT SATURDAY 2 APRIL 2016 ISSUE NO 19356

عيون وآذان

حضورها بارز في شوارع الشرق الأقصى

لافتات النيون "توهّج في عالم بائس"

□ انسان (كوريا الجنوبية) – ربيع عبد النور

من شوارع انسان (الحياة)

آفة عالمية مرشحة للتفاقم
البدانة تصيب ١٣٪ من البالغين

بول المدينة

فرنسي يستعد لـ"نهاية العالم"

جهاد الخازن
khazen@alhayat.com

"سولار أمبالس ٢" تحلّق مجدداً بعد أيام

الممثلة الأميركية كيري واشنطن حضرت العرض الأول لفيلم Confirmation في هوليوود. (أ ب)

Page from *Al Hayat*

The redesigned masthead with the globe behind the logotype was a significant improvement. It kept all the familiar elements in play, but with a far stronger focus. This was enhanced by a modular design layout that sticks to the grid system, maintains clean simple lines, and eliminates all of the extraneous visual clutter evident in the previous design.

The geography of a newspaper can become complicated. *Al Hayat* needed to simplify the day-to-day placements for daily items and give regular and clear signposts and directions for the reader. If there were sections or supplements, they needed to draw attention to them in the newspaper and link articles and features that were on separate pages with prominent captions. All of this needed to be done to keep the readers' attention and keep them informed. The articles were enhanced with graphics, cartoons, illustrations, and quotation panels. Balance through visual variety kept the pace fairly consistent on a day-to-day basis. Familiar with the layout and running style, readers intuitively were able to identify section variations from one another.

In altering the look of *Al Hayat*, fonts were kept to a minimum, and any variations were related by virtue of complementary styles, weights, and sizes. Consistency of typographic appearance is how a newspaper can differentiate itself from the competition. This was accomplished by defining the typefaces to be used in which sections. Set grids and measurements allowed for variations, complementing each other and working together when juxtaposed. The project allowed for variations within the set rules, but these rules could never be broken. For example, all headlines were ranged right with no exception.

With globalization, people are becoming similar in a variety of ways especially when it comes to their needs, such as comfort and lifestyle requirements. Newspapers are one of these elements that contribute to this lifestyle. Therefore, coming back to our subject, you will find that Arabic newspapers can be treated, to an advanced level, like English or Western newspapers. That doesn't mean that they should copy the Western ones: they simply have to apply the system that they have used in order to address the readers while looking closely at cultural differences and local identity.

Al Jazirah

Meaning 'the peninsula' in Arabic, *Al Jazirah* is a daily newspaper published in Saudi Arabia. Established in 1960, the paper has developed from a weekly to a daily and has embraced the same technological changes that all media outlets have had to face in the digital age. In 1996 the newspaper was the first in Saudi Arabia to launch an online edition. Since then, it has launched more websites dedicated to youth culture, women, real estate, and automobiles. Moreover, *Al Jazirah* introduced applications like *Al Jazirah* Snap, *Al Jazirah* Plus, and *Al Jazirah* Mobile.

When *Al Jazirah* updated its printing technologies, it permitted the newspaper to feature a fifth colour and also apply printed scent coatings on advertisements. In light of all these changes, *Al Jazirah* decided to rebrand and redesign. It commissioned Boutros to design a new range of typefaces for the newspaper's headlines and another range for its body text.

The headline fonts fused traditional and contemporary design concepts in line with *Al Jazirah*'s strategic approach of keeping up with the times while honouring cultural traditions. The typeface simplifies the calligraphic strokes of Naskh and widens the counters to allow more white space within and between characters, and it comes in three weights, regular, bold and extra bold. This same approach was used for the body text, which was designed to complement the headline face. Boutros Jazirah Text is a modern adaptation of the classical Naskh script, and it was meticulously crafted for optimal readability in newspaper body text setting.

1960 — 1964 — 1964 — 1972

ثاني أكبر تاجر عملات في العالم ينصح المضاربين:

ابقوا بعيداً عن الريال السعودي.. فلديهم العديد من المصادر غير المستغلة للتمويل !

العاصمة - «الجزيرة»

نصح «دويتشة بنك» ثاني أكبر تاجر عملة في العالم في تقرير له المضاربين، بالإبقاء بعيدا عن الريال السعودي، مشيرا إلى أن لدى السعودية العديد من المصادر غير المستغلة للتمويل.

وبحسب «بلومبرج» فقد أشار «دويتشة بنك» في تقريره إلى أن لدى المملكة احتياطات كافية للدفاع عن ربط عملتها بالدولار، ويجب على المستثمرين انتظار الوصول إلى مستويات أفضل قبل الشراء بعقود آجلة مدتها 12 شهرا، وفقا لتقرير أصدره دويتشة بنك.

وأضاف «إن السعوديين لديهم العديد من المصادر غير المستغلة للتمويل باستخدام الدولار، أحدها إصدار دين بالدولار». وكان الدين أكثر ارتفاعا والاحتياطات أقل بكثير خلال فترة الدفاعات

المملكة قد تخفض قيمة عملتها للمرة الأولى

الناجحة ما بين 1998 و2003».

في حين انخفضت احتياطات النقد الأجنبي لأكبر الدول المصدرة للنفط في العالم للشهر العاشر على التوالي حتى شهر تشرين الثاني، لتصل إلى أكثر من 600 مليار دولار، وهو رقم يساوي حجم ميزانية المملكة العربية السعودية قد تعرضت

الناتج المحلي الإجمالي للمملكة العربية السعودية، وفقا للبنك.

وقال التقرير: إن تخفيض قيمة العملة لن يعيد القدرة التنافسية للمملكة، حيث يهيمن النفط على الصادرات ويجعل من جلب العمالة والمواد أكثر تكلفة، بحسب الاقتصادي السعودي ملهم الملهم.

وارتفعت يوم الجمعة الماضي العقود الآجلة التي مدتها 12 شهرا والمرتبطة بالريال إلى أعلى مستوى منذ ديسمبر 1996 يوم الجمعة، مما يعكس تزايد التكهنات بأن المملكة قد تخفض قيمة عملتها للمرة الأولى في ثلاثة عقود.

وقد تعهدت المملكة فإن سلطة تثبيت عملات عمان والبحرين سيكون أكثر صعوبة من تثبيت عملة المملكة العربية السعودية.

ضغوط بعد انخفاض أسعار النفط، المصدر الرئيسي للدخل في البلاد، إلى أدنى مستوياتها منذ عام 2004.

وأعلنت المملكة عن خطط لخفض النفقات والإعانات للتعامل مع هذا التراجع وربما باستقلال أسواق الدين المحلية والدولية هذا العام لتمويل العجز. وبحسب تقرير بنك دويتشة فإن

Above: Al Jazirah's newly commissioned Boutros Jazirah Headline (in three weights) and Boutros Jazirah Text (in two weights)

Below: Al Jazirah's evolution over the 20th century

1975   1979   1982   1992

Old layout and font (2015)

New layout and font (2016)

Type Design for TV:
Al Arabiya

In the wake of 11 September, Arabic speakers needed an international media outlet that could best serve the Arab community without totally discounting the international community. *Al Arabiya* News Network was born. As the world's first Arab news channel prepared to launch, much consideration was given to the network's corporate identity. At its core, *Al Arabiya* sought to facilitate a fair, impartial dialogue within various Arab communities and the Western world. The real challenge for the network was to incorporate graphic aspects of Western news culture without, as most Arabs saw it, the biased content that plagued much of Western news coverage.

The brief was clear and stated that the network required an overall design sensibility that accommodated all facets of reporting the news, both in print and through the low-resolution medium of television. *Al Arabiya* needed more than just a logo; it needed an entire typeface that could be used in all capacities of reporting the news from maps, tables and graphs, to scrolling breaking news that runs across the bottom of the screen.

Commissioned from Boutros™ through the London-based agency Lambie Nairn, both logotype and the unique Arabic typeface achieved this balance and demonstrated the need to incorporate traditional aspects of Arabic typography with graphic design elements of the contemporary global community. For example, the network wanted to stress its balanced broadcasting of the news in order to establish international credibility, thus the creation of the network's clean-cut logo.

After much research and considerable testing for legibility, style and weight balance, it was decided that the typeface now conveyed internal consistency and harmony of type when compared to the equivalent Latin typeface. From a typographic point of view, this was accomplished through a geometric style that adhered to Arabic dimensions found in Arabic calligraphic style but taking into account the limitations of televised images. Rendering the created type as such gave it a cultural legacy and a direct link to traditional Arabic heritage. The added modernity came to exemplify how new Arabic typefaces can be created in the context of the modern world enjoying an up-to-date look and high-technical quality without forfeiting the essence of Arabic, and its strong cultural foundations.

Hence, writers and reporters could work directly with the graphics without the need for a graphic operator, speeding up the delivery of news on-air. In addition, the typeface had to have relatively short ascenders and descenders since it had to sit within graphic layouts built with narrow strips of colour. The font had to be developed with more than one weight since the aim was to allow the Arabic typography to create various impacts. And, finally, achieving proper alignment of the Arabic text was another challenge since the editing software used in the newsroom did not fully support the Arabic language.

The final result was a simple distinguished style that fulfilled the network's visual needs.

Rebranding *Al Arabiya*

Today, the potential audience for an Arabic television news channel has been estimated at between forty and fifty million. Some of these will be regular viewers although most will be less loyal, with a huge number of channels at their disposal. When *Al Arabiya* launched in 2003, it sought to tap into this vast market and rapidly became one of the top pan-Arab television news channels. Almost five years after its initial launch, the network decided to rebrand its Arabic typography corporate identity.

Al Arabiya continues to attract viewers through its combination of fast-breaking news stories, authoritative analysis, intelligent business programming, and balanced reporting. *Al Arabiya* also acts as a catalyst for proper dialogue within the different cultures of the Arabic-speaking world and between those cultures and the West.

From the very beginning, a strong corporate identity was necessary to communicate the channel's integrity and balanced broadcasting and to reflect its character and vision. Five years on, *Al Arabiya* wanted a more contemporary look with the objective of attracting new viewers, without alienating the existing audience. *Al Arabiya*'s new identity also needed to stand out from the competition and communicate with its audience of sophisticated media consumers with ease.

Fadi Radi, senior news graphic designer, explains: 'The brief looked like this: *Al Arabiya* graphics should reflect clarity, transparency and should keep up with the speed of news. This is what we worked on and eventually achieved, through developing a clean white logo reflecting the clear aspect of the channel and keeping the link between the old Arabic calligraphic style and modern Arabic TV typography. That was the first step of many towards the complete font package that *Al Arabiya* is now using. *Al Arabiya*'s special font was the next logical and integral part in the building of *Al Arabiya*'s image. We were looking for a geometric style that preserved the Arabic dimensions, but that had to be legible on low-resolution devices such as the TV screen.

مبادرات السلام العربية
مبادرات السلام العربية

The new unique, rebranded range of typefaces. The design was created taking into consideration the final look on the TV screen using the latest technology as well as suitability for print media (with all the attendant technical implications) in order to achieve the best results. The legibility, style, and weight balance were meticulously studied so as to achieve internal consistency and harmony with the equivalent Latin typeface. The other major characteristics that were considered used interpretations of classic Arabic fonts giving a touch of authenticity as well as modernity. The new typefaces are clean, simple, softer and visually appealing, reinforcing the reputation of the MBC group and retaining the aesthetic properties of Arabic calligraphy.

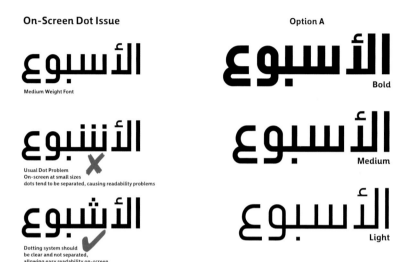

On-Screen Dot Issue

Medium Weight Font

Usual Dot Problem
On-screen at small sizes
dots tend to be separated, causing readability problems

Dotting system should
be clear and not separated,
allowing easy readability on-screen

Option A

Bold

Medium

Light

'The result was the first Arabic font to be designed specifically for such an application. Another consideration was to have a font with graphic appeal, so that it could be used by writers and reporters without the need for a graphic operator, thus allowing faster on-air information delivery when needed. As a result, the Crawler system was built with the accuracy and speed required by the channel and capable of delivering breaking news in the appropriate style in a very short period of time.'

Al Arabiya has the largest news studio in the Arabic-speaking world and is fully automated in order to give the designers more time to be creative. The revised brand identity was designed to reflect these aspects by being

both modern and credible. All the relevant elements, from the logotype to the specially developed Arabic font, were redesigned (without deviating too much from what is today the standard Arabic TV typography).

The channel's image strategy was to avoid on-screen effects and focus on the message. As previously noted, developing a font with more than one weight increased its impact. The font design, therefore, had to deliver that powerful yet simple image. Throughout the font development stages, tests on the new automated system were carried out and many changes and amendments were made in order to achieve the look that precisely reflected the channel's spirit.

BBC Arabic

BBC News, the world's largest international news broadcaster, is highly respected for the quality of its journalism, integrity, and trustworthiness. But in an increasingly multimedia world, it faced a number of significant challenges because audience loyalty was no longer guaranteed, forcing the brand to work even harder for its market share.

The proliferation of twenty-two BBC News brands resulted in misattribution, with audiences often unaware they were actually viewing BBC News. The new visual identity needed to unify BBC News's output – demonstrating greater coherence across the portfolio on a global basis and thereby enhancing their presence locally, regionally, and globally, aligning all BBC journalism to the BBC News brand. The brand needed to stand out in an increasingly competitive marketplace – while at the same time, respect the character and individuality of different output areas.

BBC's Arabic TV was part of a broader project to redefine the Arabic Service and its relationship with its audience, defining the mission as follows: 'To launch a competitive and distinctive Arabic TV Channel as part of a multi-media offer from the BBC's Arabic Service thus enabling audiences to access BBC News in Arabic through the distribution method of their choice.'

Of the estimated audience of 45 million potential BBC Arabic TV viewers, many of those people were regular viewers of competing channels. A much larger number were lighter consumers of news, relying on general channels to deliver their news. The viewers were sophisticated media consumers. They had a vast number of TV channels via satellite to choose from, regularly comparing and contrasting their options.

The BBC's brand value across the Arabic-speaking world is one of trusted, impartial news and information, but the brand is also identified as older and more traditional. With the TV launch, the Arabic Service was looking to refresh this identity with a more modern appeal to attract a new audience, while not alienating an existing one.

تبادل تجاري ضخم بينهما

خروج بريطانيا من الاتحاد الأوروبي
الآلاف يتظاهرون في وسط لندن رفضا للخروج بعد الاستفتاء الذي جرى الأسبوع الماضي
محافظ بنك إنجلترا يلمح إلى | اقتصاد | 22:01 GMT مع اليهودية في الضفة الغربية | BBC عربي

The BBC knew that identifying its brand through calligraphic elements was vital to build 'the reputation of the BBC Arabic Service as a guardian of the Arabic language'. Recognizing the importance of drawing on calligraphic traditions while also allowing for a font capable of onscreen treatments that would work across a rolling news channel, on website headers, and as an identifying element on all off-screen prints showed how keenly aware the BBC was of Arabic and the populations that speak Arabic.

The brief from the BBC made clear that the Arabic font would appear on screen in three weights and had to be designed to be situated beside or below the English BBC logo (inside the tile). It had to be compatible, being used in titles of programmes and news; for information straps giving names of contributors; and for the news scrolling across the bottom of the screen. The font needed to be clearly readable in all of these applications, as well as being instantly recognizable.

Doha TV

Qatar National Day Celebration and TV Channel

Started in 2007, Qatar's National Day, observed on 18 December, celebrates Sheikh Jassem bin Mohamed al Thani, the founder of the state of Qatar. For the 2008 festivities, a television station was created to promote, for only one week, Qatari culture around the Middle East. Broadcasting on Nilesat, Hotbird, and Arabsat, the programming combined live National Day celebrations, documentaries, talk shows, and news bulletins – covering both modern and traditional aspects of Qatar.

This channel required full visual branding, including channel and programme identities, a news package, and on-screen presentation graphics. As the channel was to be on-air for just a week, the branding solution needed to achieve both high impact and an instant association with Qatar, showcasing the nation's many unique qualities. Additionally, the channel was intended to appeal to visitors and business audiences alike. As such, its content encompassed a wide range of topics – from heritage, tourism, and sport to business, industry, and education.

Most of the station's programming would be live action, so animation was identified as a cost-effective means of showcasing the scheduled content. The resulting designs created a rich, illustrated world rooted in Qatar's national colours of maroon and white. A triangle from the Qatari flag became a graphic pattern-making device, morphing into the channel's logo. The series of images identifying the channel portrays emblematic scenes of Qatar, from the deserts and traditional souks to the modern skylines and sporting arenas. This solution utilized the creative possibilities of animation, while seamlessly integrating film.

Because the channel was temporary, there is no viewing data. However, anecdotally the channel was very well received and the National Day Organizing Committee was extremely pleased with the solution. Philippe Chapon, the channel's creative manager, said, 'We needed a creative idea for the channel crafted to a high standard, yet be cost effective and delivered in a short timescale . . . [and this] was achieved.'

Abu Dhabi TV

Abu Dhabi TV (ADTV) had a history of success and was well respected throughout the Arabic-speaking world. However, with the region's free-to-air channels exploding from twenty to 370, the fight for audience share became more and more of a struggle. As a consequence, the competition for advertising revenue was increasingly tough. But, with very few of the region's channels offering a distinct experience, ADTV recognized the opportunity to reassert its position in the marketplace and re-establish its brand in the minds of viewers.

The goal was to create a brand identity for ADTV that embodied its ambition to strike a perfect balance between a strong respect for cultural heritage and the very real aspiration to provide the highest quality in programming that would appeal to a range of audiences. Because the Abu Dhabi TV brand featured three unique channels – Abu Dhabi One, Abu Dhabi Sport, and Abu Dhabi Al Emarat – it was decided that the creation of a core broadcaster brand would create synergy across the portfolio of channels.

This core broadcaster brand took the form of 'Arabian Ambition', expressed via distinctive visual identities and on-screen presentation graphics. The new logo featured a sparkling multifaceted diamond, enabling the creation of a visual language for the family of brands.

Each channel stands on its own, but brought together they provide the strength of the brand. This concept also took the future into account, leaving room for new channels. Since the rebranding, ADTV 1 is now among the top-five stations in its category, having been among the top ten. The broadcaster has seen a significant rise in ratings and a dramatic increase in advertising, including spots for PepsiCo, Procter & Gamble, and Reckitt Benckiser.

Al Arab TV

Al Arab News Channel fills a critical void in Arabic-language news programming by delivering millions of viewers with an objective, fresh, and unbiased view of local and world events. The channel features extensive news programming as well as travel, politics, social affairs, sports, and culture coverage, and the channel's partnership with Bloomberg makes it the reference point for the region's business community.

ART TV

The brief for this project required that a brand identity was created for this Middle East television network and its range of programming from sports to Arabic films and situational comedies.

The new typeface kept in mind the network's original logo, but was made simpler so as to communicate its range of programming to all its audiences. The result was a design template into which any brand of programming could fit while always maintaining the network's brand identity.

Basic Arabic

Basic Arabic is a typeface design influenced by the possibility of matching aspects of Latin typography with new Arabic typefaces. In 1947 the Lebanese architect and typographer Nasri Khattar made one of the earliest and most significant attempts in this endeavour. The stylistic characteristics of this attempt were as follows:

- The reduction of the number of shapes per letter
- The reduction of the diacritic dots
- The inclusion of the Arabic accents in the alphabet as extra letters
- The normalization of the letterform and the augmentation of the central height.

The major flaws in Khattar's design were the lack of consideration for the proportions of the letterforms and the reluctance to utilize the potential of traditional calligraphic styles.

With that said, the result was more than acceptable: it was satisfying. It also proved the flexibility of Arabic letterforms, although Arabic typographic culture had yet to fully embrace this design trait.

Basic Arabic resulted from the same desire to blend characteristics of Latin and Arabic typography with the added twist of teaching Arabic to Arab children. When learning to read English and French, children are taught to read the twenty-six letters of the Latin alphabet as one basic shape. They are also taught to read and write the characters at the same time. The addition of cursive presents very little difficulty because the youngsters can already read the alphabet. It is a matter of a few more shapes. In other words, children learning English or French start with simple letters, and then move on to more complicated ones, eventually able to understand and use four different letterforms: the capital and lowercase letters used for print, and the capital and lowercase letters used for cursive.

لبط طلب بطل طبل

Unified Arabic Neo-Naskhi

ملك لكم كله كما

Unified Arabic Kufic

بدر درب ردب دبر

Unified Arabic Beiruti

بزق بقر قرب قبر رقب

Unified Arabic Al-Raya

Examples of Nasri Khattar's Unified Arabic ranges

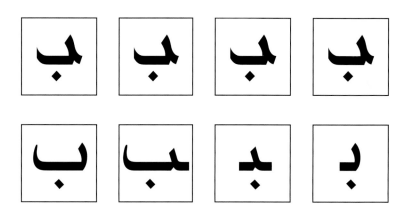

In the Middle East, the programme for teaching children to read Arabic requires two years. It may take another two or three years before children can write it correctly. The reasons for this are varied, and extend beyond the scope of the creation of Basic Arabic. For the sake of this case study, however, the point that needs to be kept in mind is that prior to Basic Arabic the creation of new Arabic typefaces depended heavily on handwritten calligraphy and did not use the technological advances of the printing press.

The printing press created two great advantages over handwriting and block printing. It could reproduce printed pages, and therefore books, in a fraction of the time needed for either of the other methods. In other words, the invention of the printing press liberated writing from handwriting or calligraphy. It did not abolish it but added another dimension to writing.

Not long after the invention of the printing press in Germany, another innovation was made in France: the letters that the typesetter composed were no longer based on the cursive handwritten style, but were simplified and standardized; they were designed as 'type', and the art of typography was born. Arabs, however, were reluctant to adopt the distinction between print and handwriting, insisting that printed words should imitate handwritten words.

As a response to these issues, Basic Arabic's design was related directly to the shape of the letters. The first step in the design process was to simplify the different shapes of the same letter by creating one shape for every Arabic letter, and using that single shape no matter where it was positioned in the word. Standardizing the shapes did not deny the calligraphic origins of the language, maintaining elements of the Naskh style, the most popular serif typeface with a traditional look.

Another aspect of Basic Arabic's flexibility that spans Latin and Arabic typography is its ability to be connected in the traditional way of writing Arabic or disconnected as is the way of the Latin alphabet. The economy of space provided by the typeface is also very important, especially since it was an integral part of its design. Tests revealed that Basic Arabic decreased the need for page space by 15 to 20 per cent so a dictionary of 1,000 pages could carry the same information using only 800.

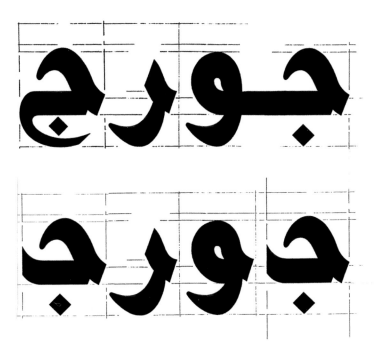

رايـة المعـرب

السادات أحرق الجسور مع السوفيات ووضع كل البيض في السلة الأميركية

رايـة المعـرب

السادات أحرق الجسور مع السوفيات ووضع كل البيض في السلة الأميركية

Basic Arabic decreased the need for page space by 15 to 20 per cent.

In summary, the main objectives of Basic Arabic are:

- To open the way for creative Arabic typography that follows the scientific design principles governing typography in the rest of the world.
- To facilitate the process of teaching Arabic-speaking children and adults to read and write in Arabic.
- To facilitate learning to read Arabic and to use the Arabic alphabet in their own languages – e.g. Urdu – for non-Arabic speaking peoples, particularly in Muslim countries.
- To introduce the Basic Arabic method into the publishing media gradually in order to familiarize the reading public with the idea.
- To demonstrate the commercial advantages of using Basic Arabic as a scientifically designed typeface that enables important economies of space and paper.

Basic Arabic in use as a headline for a magazine

5 Designing with Arabic

This clock face demonstrates the flexibility of Arabic calligraphy. It reads 'Parmigiani' from all angles in a modern geometrical style; the falcon is designed in a freehand style, made to repeat the word 'Parmigiani' in Arabic. The colours black, red, green, and white represent Arab culture, as does the gold, which represents the desert.

Exploring Samples of Arabic Typography

The following pages are dedicated to showing examples of designs using Arabic that are corporate and non-corporate. The great value of looking at examples of various graphic applications of Arabic commissioned by high-profile companies is that such projects often have access to expensive resources, whether talent or technology. With that said, the merit of all these examples in terms of design is equal to that of the case studies about the *Al Arabiya* television network or the creation of Basic Arabic.

Whether a book jacket, a student-designed poster or contemporary calligraphy created for the sake of art, the examples in the gallery prove the extent to which Arabic can be experimented with and modified without losing the written language's illustrious history. By studying the basic elements of the language's typographic past and emulating the innovative approaches of these contemporary designs, the potential of designing with Arabic will quickly be realized.

Commercial Bank of Qatar

The rebranding of the four-crescent logo of the Commercial Bank of Qatar was individually crafted for both Arabic- and English-speaking customers. The uppercase logotype worked in harmony with its Arabic variant, and subtle details were shared between each language version. The inclusion of the tear on the 'C' in the English font is influenced by the descender found in the *ya* character in Arabic. The use of sharp vertical and horizontal forms of the Arabic word were crafted to reflect the rigid nature of the uppercase English variant. The density of the variants was carefully balanced in the line weights and character spaces to create the ideal visual symmetry.

Boutros Arlette & tajawal

Named after the Arabic word *tajawal*, meaning to wander or roam, tajawal is an online travel platform founded in April 2015 that aims to dominate the travel market in the Middle East and North Africa region by providing a world-class mobile and online travel booking experience.

To understand why Boutros Arlette is used, we have to understand the branding concept behind tajawal. The tajawal branding concept is broken down to the foundations of design and travel. To reflect the youthful and dynamic personality of the brand, the logo is taken apart into geometric shapes, which are the fundamentals of design. These colourful shapes are arranged to point in different directions, indicating the growth of tajawal – travelling in all directions and limitless (beyond flights, hotels, and other travel products). Once arranged together, these shapes turn into a modern-day compass: the logo, a dropped pin, informs the traveller of where they are in the world.

رحلات جوية وفنادق حول العالم

Flights and hotels from **around the world**

Boutros Arlette Arabic and Latin in five weights

Boutros Arlette used by tajawal

Boutros Arlette used by tajawal

Boutros MINI Arabic

A range of typefaces were created by Arlette Boutros in collaboration with Serviceplan Middle East. The brief was to create a range of inline Arabic typefaces to harmonize with the characteristics of the existing MINI Latin range of typefaces.

For the headline range (in four weights), Boutros supplied a range that works in harmony with the existing MINI Latin range. When developing such ranges, Boutros always makes sure that the typeface design works well with its equivalent Latin counterpart in style and weight, and for its complete legibility. After all, the main aim is to create a typeface to communicate a clear message while retaining intact its Arabic calligraphic and cultural feel.

For the body text range (in two weights), Boutros had to consider the serif ending of most of the characters and reduce it to the minimum, as well as redesigning some of the characters such as the medial *ain* to ensure that it did not look like the medial *feh*. All these treatments make the typeface very legible at a small point size.

Boutros MINI is the font of choice for a broad range of corporate and individual multilingual applications including online and offline media.

تستقبلك على الرحب والسعة.

ALL THE SPACE YOU NEED.

Boutros MINI Arabic and Latin

تستقبلك على الرحب والسعة.

www.mini-dubai.com

MINI CLUBMAN الجديدة.
عبّر بشغف.

اتصل بمركز الاتصال الخاص بالمركز الميكانيكي للخليج العربي على الرقم: (2462) 800-AGMC
أو راسلنا إلكترونياً على العنوان: campaign@agmc.ae أو تفضل بزيارة صالات عرض MINI في شارع
الشيخ زايد في دبي، والمنطقة الصناعية 12، الشارع 3 في الشارقة.
المركز الميكانيكي للخليج العربي - عضو في مجموعة البطحاء للسيارات.

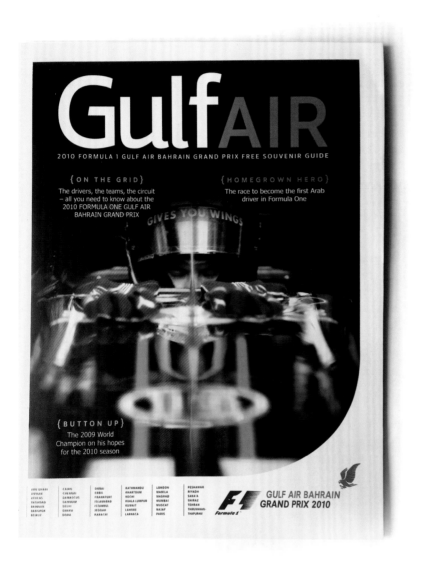

Tanseek in use in *Gulf Air* magazine

Tanseek in use by MBC Drama

With the aim to create a visual communication impact as well as improve driving conditions on the road leading up to the Khalil Gibran Museum in Bcharré, Lebanon – birthplace of the author of *The Prophet* – various quotations were selected from the poet's writings and illustrated by a group of selected artists, designers, and typographers. The final execution was delivered by engraving the designs using composite panels lit from the back by a warm LED light that adjusts brightness depending on the time of day.

The Arabic quotation reads: 'Pity the nation that is full of beliefs and empty of religion.'

Signage at the Khalil Gibran Museum in Bcharré, Lebanon

Converting an ad campaign from English to Arabic is not just a matter of translation. These ads were based on an international campaign in which the emphasis was placed on the circle around the letter 'M' in Motorola. The key concept of centring the ads on the events of daily life, from family to business, could not be maintained with a straight translation.

Copywriting expertise was required to match the meaning of the translation without destroying the message's concept. The challenge was finding the correct word for the headline that always started with the letter *meem* in Arabic, which is equivalent to the letter 'M' in English.

Bilingual Signage

When it comes to long-distance reading, the human eye blurs the shapes being seen, making them appear somewhat fuzzy. As a result, certain measures need to be taken when designing signage.

In designing Latin signage, the most important starting point is to ensure that all inherent typographic complexity is removed, simplifying the character shapes as much as possible to ensure maximum legibility. It goes without saying, therefore, that signage typefaces must be sans serif. They should also not be geometrical designs, in order to avoid misreading similar-looking characters. Each letterform should be seen as a whole, solid form and not as a constructed item of straight and rounded units.

Similar principles apply in the design of Arabic typeface signage. The world's most widely used – and, consequently, the most pirated – typeface for bilingual Arabic and Latin signage and wayfinding is Boutros Advertisers Naskh, designed in 1977 by Mourad and Arlette Boutros in collaboration with Letraset.

Boutros Advertisers Naskh can be seen in action on bilingual signage throughout the Arabic-speaking world, where it is used in offices and hospitals; on motorway signs; and in commercial spaces such as Dubai and Beirut international airports.

Signs in Boutros Advertisers Naskh inside and outside Dubai International Airport

مطار بيروت الدولي
Beirut Int'l Airport
↓

Released in 2016, the typeface Boutros Sign was designed using the latest technology, which was not available in 1977, with the aim of replacing the existing Boutros Advertisers Naskh with an improved bilingual typeface. Boutros Sign was designed by Arlette Boutros and Eva Masoura, who collaborated in order for the Arabic and Latin scripts to be in typographic harmony.

The typeface Boutros Sign in use

Boutros Aura, designed by Boutros Fonts / Soulaf Khalifeh, is a contemporary calligraphic style that merges features from the more classical scripts, combining the aesthetics of Naskh with the proportions of Thuluth. The display typeface has two extra stylistic sets in addition to the default one.

نكتب
الكلمات
نصنع للمعاني أقفاصاً من
وعليه، إذا كان النثر قفصاً من فضة فالشعر قفصاً
من الذهب

نصْنع للمَعانِي أقفاصاً مِنْ الكلمَات
Default Set

نصْنع للمَعاني أقفاصاً مِنْ الكلمَات
Stylistic Set 1

نصْنع للمَعاني أقفاصاً مِنْ الكلمَات
Stylistic Set 2

Boutros Asma & Almarai

The beauty of Boutros Asma lies in its clarity and simplicity. Beneath the font's geometric look lies a strict adherence to calligraphic structure and rules. Each letter was crafted with great attention to detail in order to keep subtle hints of handwriting. Letters have low contrast and wide apertures in all four weights. These characteristics were made to enhance the font's readability in various media, especially on screen, making it a suitable choice for the corporate font of Almarai, the leading Saudi dairy company.

Boutros Asma can be seen on Almarai's website, in their stores, and across their social media, creating a distinctive brand image (see pp.150–53).

خط بطرس أسمى
من مجموعة خطوط بطرس العربية

Light — قطعت المراعي شوطا كبيرا من التوسع والتطوير منذ أن استشعر صاحب السمو الأمير

Regular — سلطان بن محمد بن سعود الكبير في عام ١٩٧٧، أهمية تطوير صناعة الألبان في المملكة

Bold — العربية السعودية وبرؤية واضحة قوامها الجودة كمعيار لتقديم أطعمة متميزة، أصبحت

ExtraBold — المراعي اليوم أكبر شركة متكاملة رأسياً لمنتجات الألبان في العالم لتثرى حياة

تنتج المراعي أكثر من
٢٤ نكهة من العصائر

#حقائق_عن_المراعي

www.almarai.com

Almarai has taken on Boutros Asma as their corporate font.

ابن النفيس
عالم عربي موسوعي

عالم موسوعي وطبيب عربي مسلم
يعد مكتشف الدورة الدموية الصغرى
وأحد رواد علم وظائف الأعضاء
عين رئيساً لأطباء مصر
ويعتبره كثيرون أعظم فيزيولجيّ لعصور الوسطى

الميلاد: ١٢١٣، دمشق، سوريا
الوفاة: ١٢٨٨، القاهرة، مصر

www.almarai.com

Al Sakhra, Cliff House, Beirut, is an authentic Lebanese restaurant open since 1936. In 2016 an identity uplift was undertaken to give a fresh and contemporary look rooted in tradition.

Bilingual communication materials for a New Zealand export company

Qatalum is a joint venture between Qatar Petroleum and Norsk Hydro.

VIP ماركة 🏵 MARKA VIP

Arabic logo adaptation for Marka VIP

كلاتونز
CLUTTONS

Arabic logo adaptation for a property group

Custom logo for Ali Zaid Al Quraishi & Brothers (AZAQ), a leading business group in Saudi Arabia and the region.

This is a logotype for the women's body spray Farasha: *farasha* means butterfly in English. Written in a Diwani calligraphic style, it clearly looks like a butterfly, once again showcasing the flexibility of Arabic creative calligraphy.

The logo for Elaf, a travel company that specializes in pilgrimage tours. Notice the Latin 'E' in the lower right corner for the first Latin letter in the company's name.

Global

ADVOCACY AND
LEGAL COUNSEL

Arabic logo using a calligraphy bamboo for a UAE law firm

BedoInn

The name of this UAE-based lifestyle brand is a pun on Bedouin, desert-dwelling nomads. It is worth noting how the logo's shades of red and orange speak to the desert landscape.

Arabic logotype conversion for UAE landscaping company TerraVerde

Arabic and English logos for Sanctuary Cay – an exclusive spa experience

This burger chain in Beirut, Lebanon, has logos in English and Arabic that complement one another visually.

ZMOROD

This calligraphic logo for a restaurant in Aleppo, Syria, is in Diwani Jali.

Omaymatee, a restaurant in Riyadh, Saudi Arabia, is in the Diwani style.

ش.م.م

hbr s.a.r.l
creative platform

Co-founded by Nelly Baz and Halim Choueiry, hbr is a design workspace dedicated to manifesting conceptual innovation into physical product. Utilizing the latest technology and equipment, design services on offer include, but are not limited to, corporate gifts, digital designs, plaques, signs (both outdoors and indoors), novel light fixtures, writing boards, and customized display units.

DESIGNED IN LEBANON

The aim of {Designed in Lebanon} is to empower Lebanese designers through an apprenticeship programme. The founders of {Designed in Lebanon} come from multidisciplinary backgrounds, which allow them to design systems rather than aesthetics. This inclusive platform believes in collective intelligence, therefore it depends on designers to work interdependently with other designers and organizations in order to turn the hbr creative platform into a living lab.

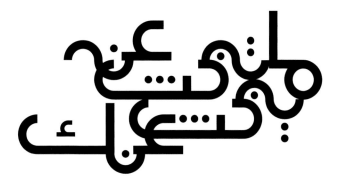

These contemporary geometrical styles, which depict two proverbs, look more like illustrations than lettering.

Top: 'What you look for is looking for you.'
Above: 'As you condemn, you will be condemned.'

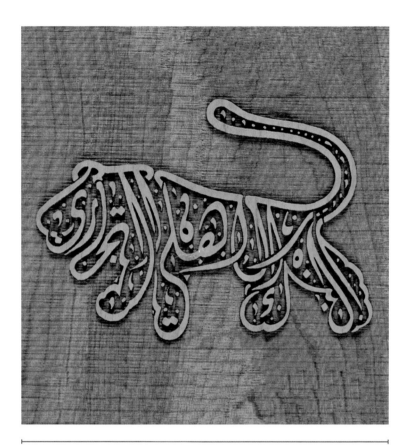

A logo for the National Commercial Bank where the bank wanted a logo that matched their motto: 'Rooted in the past, banking for the future.' Shaped like a lion in the Diwani style, the logo clearly conveys the idea that the bank is the leader of the pack.

A bilingual logo for the International Arab Horse Racing Club based in the UAE

A bilingual Latin-Arabic logo in the shape of a belly dancer. While the English reads Belly Queen the Arabic reads '*Ahlam Asharq*', which means 'the dreams of the East'.

Converting logotypes is about more than forcing letters to fit into the same space. One important factor is implementing fonts that complement the originals and thus provide graphic continuity.

The Arabic translates as: 'Bosch – Technology for Life'.

With offices throughout the Middle East, the British Council needed an Arabic logo that matched the visual feel of the English logo.

Dhikr App

Available to download on the App Store

Dhikr is an app designed as a reminder of *dhikr* (remembrance of God). It consists of
four devotional prayers. Each phrase comes in five different calligraphic styles designed
specifically for this app. The user has the freedom to customize each artwork by changing
the colour scheme and share it on social networks.

5•DESIGNING WITH ARABIC

The Qur'anic Garden identity is a collaboration between Mourad Boutros and Halim Choueiry. Commissioned by the Qatar Foundation, the Qur'anic Garden is a botanical dome grouping all the flora that are named in the Qur'an.

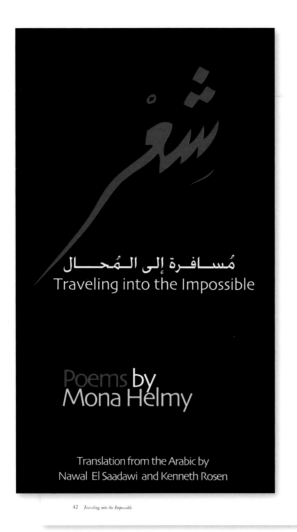

The red Arabic calligraphy on this book of bilingual Arabic and English poetry translates as 'poem'. This was the first of Litterae Mundi Translatae's short-lived publishing endeavours.

The primary objective of Litterae Mundi Translatae – a US-based publishing programme that brought quality literature from around the world to English readers – was to engage in questions of language, translation, and multiculturalism. For this reason, multicultural issues were a reality of every project. In particular, their first book, an Arabic-English volume of poetry, made the importance of these issues very clear. The challenge was the obvious dilemma of typesetting English and Arabic on the same page, bringing together two different languages read from two different directions.

Litterae Mundi Translatae contracted an expert in multilingual typography and design in order to ensure the poems achieved a balance between readability and correct presentation in both languages. Because of the cultural and religious nuances of Arabic, placing the two texts next to one another was much more of a challenge. Even with its worldly views, the publishing house knew it needed expert help in order to best represent the poetry of the two languages.

For the book's cover, many concepts were presented, all of which shared the same objective. Some were illustrated, some were strictly typographic, and some were a mixture of illustration and typography. In one example, the author's name was written in the shape of a butterfly, symbolizing freedom, beauty, youth, and femininity. Another concept showed a pen from which ink flowed, gradually transforming into a butterfly. Neither of these ideas was accepted because in Egypt (the author's home), unlike in the West, a butterfly has a negative connotation. The final version of the cover is the word 'poem' written in freehand Arabic calligraphy; the way the pen travels freely from the top to the bottom of the page says it all from the points of view of both typography and culture.

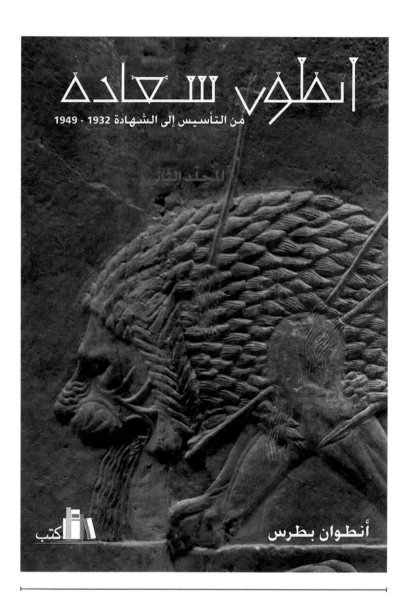

أنطون سعادة

من التأسيس إلى الشهادة 1932 - 1949

المجلد الثاني

كتب

أنطوان بطرس

The cover for this book about Lebanese philosopher, author, and politician Antoun Saadeh uses Arabic calligraphy rendered in the style of cuneiform script.

Book cover design for the Arabic translation of Johann Christoph Arnold's *Their Name Is Today: Reclaiming Childhood in a Hostile World*.

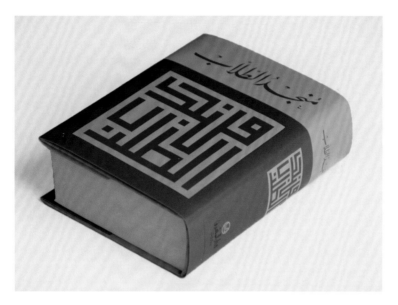

Top: Book jacket design for *Mounged al Toullab* using square Kufi calligraphy

Above: Book jacket design for *Mounged al Abjadi* in Thuluth style

5•DESIGNING WITH ARABIC

Abha Bilad Asir

Calligraphy has been a vital means of visual expression because figurative arts are not allowed under strict interpretations of Islam. Though it is the subject of the book shown here, the designer had to come up with a way to convey the subject matter without a direct visual reference. The solution was to design this calligraphy that encompasses ideas of life, marriage, childbirth, and death.

The *ayah* (verse) is the second one of *Surat Al-Mulk*, which is the *surah* number 67 (chapter 67) of the Qur'an. Its translation is 'Who has created death and life that He may test you which of you is best in deed. And He is the All-Mighty, the Oft-Forgiving.'

With this design, Apple honoured the traditions of Arabic writing while maintaining strong brand identity.

5•DESIGNING WITH ARABIC

Published in London, *Ad-Diplomasi* is the most distinguished Middle Eastern monthly news report.

Al Hayat. C'est la vie.

في الحقيقة لـم نطلـق اسـم الحيـاة على «الحياة» صـدفة.
يومياً أخبار الحياة في «الحياة». تنقـل اليكـم كل الأحـداث التـي
ترتبـط بحيـاتكـم اليـومية وتنقـلكـم إليهـا.
وكمـا تقطـع النحلـة ٨٠٠ كـلم فـي عمـرها (٣٠ الـى ٤٠ يومـاً)
لتنتج ٥ غرامـات مـن العسـل، هكـذا «الحياة» تسعـى وراء الهـم
والمثيـر والمفيـد مـن الأخبـار، حلوهـا ومـرّهـا تـراقبهـا، تفسّـرهـا
تحـلّلهـا، تفضّـلهـا ... وتقدمهـا إليكـم كـل صبـاح.

www.alhayat.com

The intention of this bee ad developed for the daily Pan-Arab newspaper *Al Hayat* is to
parallel the industriousness of the bee to the editorial voice of the paper.

Al Hayat. C'est la vie.

المواطنة من صميم الحياة تغذّي صحيفتنا وتنعش كل ما يتعلق بها

إبتسـم للحيـاة !... لا تهـدر المياه.
تقديرنا واحترامنا للحياة تحسينها
تفهمها حمايتها والمحافظة عليها
هذا هو هدفنا كل صباح.

Al Hayat. C'est la vie.

إبتسـم للحيـاة !...
حافـظ على نظافـة مدينتك.
www.alhayat.com

layat. C'est la vie.

إبتسـم للحيـاة !...
إقتصـد فـي الكـهـربـاء.
www.alhayat.com

A series of public awareness ads published in *Al Hayat* where the combination of Latin and Arabic typography and words are in harmony. *Al Hayat* means 'The Life', which the ad plays on by using the French phrase '*C'est la vie*'.

The Arabic reads as follows:
Top right: 'Smile at Life! Keep Your City Clean'
Top left: 'Smile at Life! Save Water'
Above: 'Smile at Life! Save Electricity'

These playing cards feature an ideal merging of design, typography, and culture. Drawing from themes found in *One Thousand and One Nights*, the faces of these characters portray the beauty of Middle Eastern features. This is contemporary design acknowledging the rich cultural history of the Arabic world.

LEVI'S BOOK OF BARNYARD ANIMALS

كلب
Kalb

Kelev

Собака
Sabaka

Hund

Perro

Cachorro

狗
Gǒu

いぬ
Inu

개
Gae

Hund

Chien

Dog

هر
Cat

Hatool

Кошка
Koshka

Katze

Gato

Gato

猫
Māo

ねこ
Neko

고양이
Go Yangee

Katt

Chat

Cat

Using GE Tasmeem, *Levi's Book of Barnyard Animals* was created to encourage multilingual learning at an early age by featuring twenty-one different animals surrounded by their names written in twelve different languages, including Arabic.

YA'ABERNIE
(يقبرني)
STANDARD
PHRASE
FROM ARABIC
MEANING
'YOU BURY ME.'

"A DECLARATION
OF LOVE, FROM ONE
PERSON TO ANOTHER,
INDICATING HOW
DIFFICULT IT WOULD
BE TO LIVE
WITHOUT THEM"

ARABS FOR BERNIE SANDERS

Arabs for Bernie Sanders #Yo2Bernie

Senator Bernie Sanders's presidential run sparked grassroots support across the United States and among diverse demographic groups, including Arab-Americans. Excitement for their candidate inspired a clever play on the standard Arabic phrase *ya'abernie* يقبرني, which literally translates as 'you bury me'. This term of endearment is used to express how difficult it would be to live without a loved one. Transliterated as 'Yo2Bernie', the slogan was rendered in a Ruq'a-style calligraphy with the familiar bold look and feel of Arab political posters.

Bilingual logotype and paper-bag design for Capboosi

Bilingual logotype design for Gmash (a fabrics brand), with the buttons used as diacritical notes over the letters.

Arabic calligraphy on the back of a truck in Lebanon

Bold typography presenting the title of this book about a political subject in a strong manner that complements the subject matter.

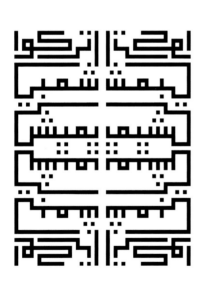

Top Left: An Arabic logo for a jewelry brand

Above: Tapestry that reads 'Let my people live' in modern Kufi geometric style.

Right: Arabic calligraphy for a jewelry design in Kufi style that reads 'My faith in God, the light of your beauty is a verse, a verse from God.'

5•DESIGNING WITH ARABIC

The personal seal of Prince Hassan Bin Talal of Jordan, written in Thuluth style in the shape of an imperial monogram, or *Tugra*.

The word *Almahaba* means love in English. This Diwani Jali style calligraphy was used on a book cover promoting a Gibran Khalil Gibran 125th-anniversary event in London at the Banqueting House in Whitehall in November 2010.

Stained-glass panels from the Aramco Mosque in Dhahran, Saudi Arabia. It is one of thirty-four panels containing the ninety-nine names of God.

5•DESIGNING WITH ARABIC

Arabic calligraphy in the Thuluth style that reads 'Say God, give me more knowledge.'

'Glory to God in the Highest. Peace on Earth and Goodwill to all Mankind.'
A privately commissioned, limited-edition print distributed as a present for Christmas and the New Year.

This translates as 'And proclaim to mankind the Hajj. They will come to you on foot and on every lean camel, they will come from every deep and distant mountain highway'. A privately commissioned, limited-edition print distributed as a present for Christmas, the New Year, and other relevant occasions.

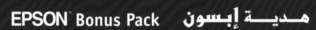

In this special Arabic Decorations CD you will find a selection of elements that will assist you in presenting your greeting cards in the best possible way at the best quality available.

There is a choice of 10 different decorative elements made of 231 items.

في هذا القرص المدمج للزخارف العربية. سوف تجدون مجموعة مختارة من العناصر التي تساعدكم في إخراج بطاقات المناسبات الخاصة بكم بأفضل صورة ممكنة وأعلى جودة متاحة. يمكنكم الاختيار من بين ١٠ عناصر للزخرفة مكونة من ٢٣١ نوعاً.

تصميـــم وإنتــاج بطـــرس إنتــــرنـاشنـال (ابـلايـد ارابيـك ليمتـد) وهـي مجموعـة مــن الخبــراء بقيـــادة مـــراد وأرليــت بطـــرس.

Designed and produced by "Boutros International" (Applied Arabic Limited), a group of experts headed by Mourad and Arlette Boutros.

In this promotional leaflet for Epson, Arabic and Latin typography and graphic ornaments work in harmony. The copy has been written and arranged in order to best balance the page.

Tattoo tiger, freehand Arabic calligraphy styled into the shape of a tiger, reading from top right downwards: *azm* (will), *kouwwa* (strength), above left: *zaka'a* (intelligence).

Arabic logo rendered to look like an eye, using an overlapping mirror image concept and Diwani Jali style calligraphy. It reads *al mushaheed*, which means 'the viewer' in English.

Commissioned by the late Guillermo Rodriguez-Benitez of San Juan, Puerto Rico, this design is for the cover of a book made of wood. Read clockwise from the right-hand corner it reads, 'Because the kingdom of God is within you.'

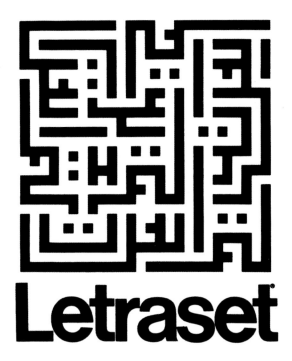

A modern take on traditional style, this shape reads 'Letraset' from every angle.

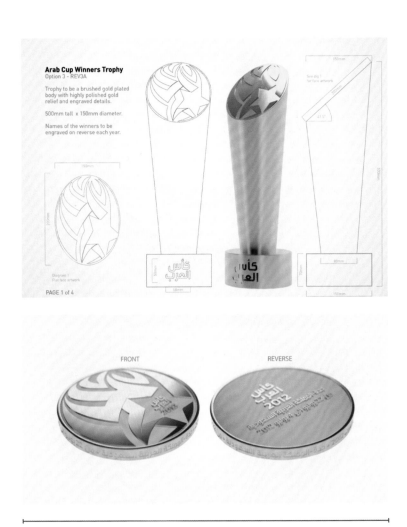

Arab Cup Medals & Trophy: A 3D creation for the Arab Cup
The design features the typeface Tanseek.

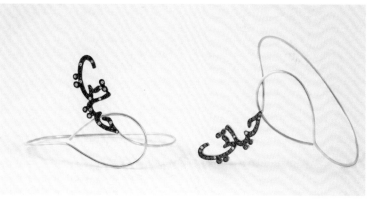

Arabic calligraphy jewelry design by award-winning jewelry designer and producer Tarfa Itani, who creates fashionable jewelry pieces made of precious stones and metals.

Title for the short film *In White* directed by Dania Bdeir

Arabic logotype design for Virgin Mobile, Qatar

6 Fine Art & Calligraphy

When love beckons to you, follow him,
Though his ways are hard and steep.
And when his wings enfold you yield to him,
Though the sword hidden among his pinions may wound you.
And when he speaks to you believe in him,
Though his voice may shatter your dreams as the north wind
lays waste the garden.

Love gives naught but itself and takes naught but from itself.
Love possesses not nor would it be possessed;
For love is sufficient unto love.

Incorporating Arabic Calligraphy

What follows are examples of collaborations between artists from all over the world, incorporating Arabic calligraphy into visual mediums, from paintings to tapestries, based on proverbs and quotations. These works exemplify how the origins of Arabic calligraphy, which has evolved during the last millennium and continues to flourish today, have spread into the realm of contemporary fine art. Using traditional skills, bamboo pens, and special inks, skilled Arabic calligraphers continue to play an important role in visual communication on an international scale, whether commissioned for international hotels or acquired by prominent collectors. Time-honoured calligraphic styles like Ruq'a, Naskhi, Ta'liq, Diwani, Thuluth, and Kufic remain core, but Arabic calligraphers today are reaching new heights of excellence. The decorative and fluid nature of Arabic lends itself to creative uses across all mediums, proving there is no shortage of ways to think about using Arabic for various visual effects.

Al Mahaba, Mourad Boutros, 2015. Oil on canvas, 70 x 50 cm

Mercy, Mourad Boutros, 2016. Oil on canvas, 75 x 100 cm. Presented by the HH Sheikh Mansoor Bin Zayed Al Nahyan Global Arabian Horse Flat Racing Festival to the Vatican.

The many and diverse religions that exist in the world are united by mercy and God is Mercy.

Inspired by the dome from the HRH Sheikh Zayed Grand Mosque and the Vatican Dome, this painting merges the two in an abstract manner to create a three-dimensional backdrop to the painting bursting into life to represent the Mercy of God. To the far right, inscriptions from the HRH Sheikh Zayed Grand Mosque provide a circular decorative framework to represent God's eternal and ever-giving grace. The colours yellow and blue represent the spiritual aspect of the painting and the heavens.

The Arabic calligraphy is a beautiful visual interpretation of 'God is Grace' (*Allah Rahma*). It uses elegant, graceful, free-flowing curves to set a smooth tone for the message in the foreground of the painting.

Miracle, Mourad Boutros, 2016. Oil on canvas, 40 x 60 cm. Presented by the HH Sheikh Mansoor Bin Zayed Al Nahyan Global Arabian Horse Flat Racing Festival to the Mayor of Rome.

In one region of the world, the sands diverged to give way to human capabilities. It was unexpected.

This painting is an interpretation of the modern-day miracle that is the UAE – a world-class achievement bursting to life from the sand in the form of a new urban, ultra-modern architectural wonder. The movement and shapes of the painting represent an abstraction of the desert transforming into a modern miracle, with the architecture and infrastructure forming a beacon across the region.

The vertical lines of life stand for the physical buildings that are ever seeking to achieve new worldwide records and landmarks. The colours represent the miracle, showing the yellow orange of the desert transforming into the new form of life, the blue background representing water. The lines around the calligraphy and it's geometric shape stand for the miraculous expansion of the UAE, heralding a new era of prosperity and growth.

Love Assigns You to his Sacred Fire, Emmanuel Guiragossian and Mourad Boutros, 2010.
Oil on canvas, 100 x 80 cm

To the Flower a Bee Is a Messenger of Love, Emmanuel Guiragossian and Mourad Boutros, 2010. Oil on canvas, 100 x 90 cm

The inspirations for this gobelin tapestry came to C.G. Schuebel after a visit to the Islamic Museum in Abu Dhabi, and also from very good friends in the Emirates, who spoke with great pride and admiration of HH Sheikh Zayed Bin Sultan Al Nahyan, of their traditions, and of their Arabian culture.

Schuebel created this very exclusive silk tapestry, woven in a masterly fashion using the most elegant of yarns. The piece is not only a homage to the Arab horse, displaying a great love for them, but also pays homage to Arab culture and tradition.

The focal point of the work is the portrait of a splendid Arab horse, whose grace and beauty immediately attracts admiring looks. The onlooker is able to sense the love and pride that every horse owner bears in the heart. The message is underlined by the brilliant calligraphy of Mourad Boutros, which Schuebel has incorporated ingeniously into her creation. The red rose stands for the great admiration and respect felt for the founder of the Emirates and for his great love of the Arab horse.

A Declaration of Love to UAE and to the Arab Horse, C.G. Schuebel, 2015. Gobelin tapestry of pure silk in a blend of natural yarns, 355 x 294 cm

Homage to the Arabian Horse of the Emirates, C.G. Schuebel, 2015. Giclée print,
60 x 179 cm

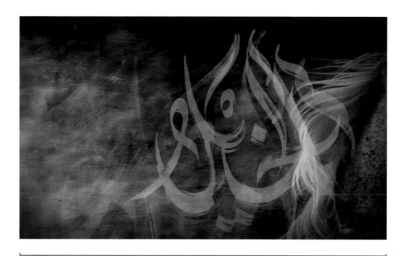

Freedom, C.G. Schuebel, 2015. Giclée print, 136 x 233 cm

6•FINE ART & CALLIGRAPHY

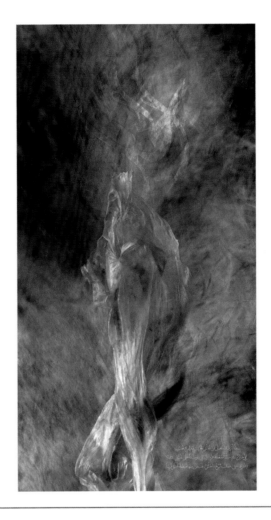

And God Said to the Wind of the Desert, C.G. Schuebel, 2015. Giclée print, 260 x 136 cm

6•FINE ART & CALLIGRAPHY

Most Arabic calligraphy by various artists is done in a variety of scripts and styles. This series by Krikor Agopian is dedicated to the Middle Eastern Arabic countries in recognition for welcoming Armenian refugees in 1915, and helping them to bloom again. In this series Agopian takes the Arabic alphabet and turns it into a work of art, treating each letter separately.

Above: *Arabic Alphabet*, Krikor Agopian and Mourad Boutros, 2015. Acrylic on canvas, 82 x 66 cm. It is part of the series dedicated to the Middle Eastern countries that welcomed Armenian refugees in 1915.

Left: *Cavalier*, Krikor Agopian and Mourad Boutros, 2015. Mixed media on canvas, 60 x 80 cm

Oum al 'Alam, Metin Salih and Mourad Boutros, 2014. Oil on canvas, 40 x 60 cm. Private commission dedicated to Her Highness Sheikha Fatima Bint Mubarak

The Horse Is the Great Pride of Every Man, Christine Saleh Jamil and Mourad Boutros, 2016. Oil on canvas, 67 x 100 cm

Founder of Aridi Computer Graphics, Inc., Lebanese-American artist Marwan Aridi's devotion to Arabic calligraphy is made clear in the specialized fonts, ornaments, and drawings he has produced over his career. All of his work stems from diligent attention to detail and a formidable knowledge of calligraphic traditions. His calligraphic creations have been commissioned for countless books, magazines, and advertisements, and exhibitions of his artwork have been held all over the world.

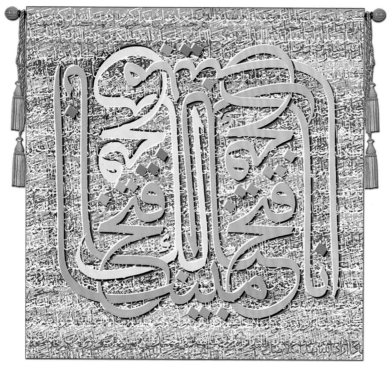

Ina Fatahna Laka, Marwan Aridi, 2015. Tapestry, 178 x 188 cm. Limited edition of 5

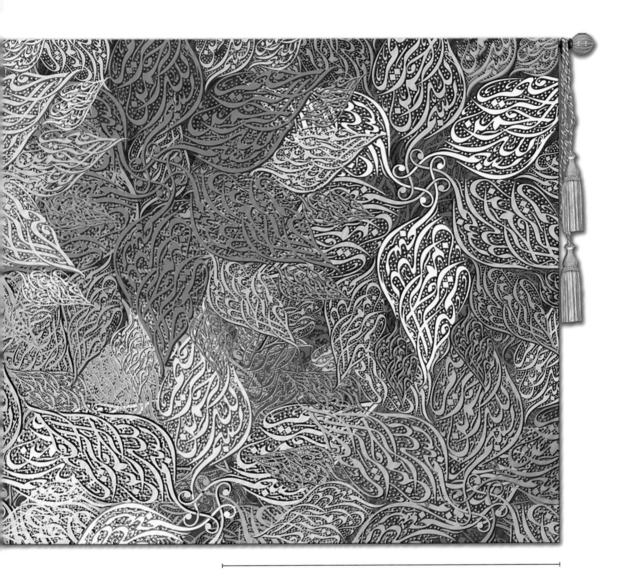

Tree of Life, Marwan Aridi, 2015. Tapestry, 134 x 180 cm. Limited edition of 5

Bibliography

Bringhurst, Robert, *The Elements of Typographic Style*. Vancouver: Hartley and Marks Publishers, 2004

Buchanan, Richard, *Branzi's Dilemma: Design in Contemporary Culture*. Design Issues 14, 1 (1998): 3–20

Esterson, Simon, 'Kit of Parts' in *Contemporary Newspaper Design*, edited by John D. Berry. New York, NY: Mark Batty Publisher, 2004

Evans, Harold, *Newspaper Graphics*. Penrose Annual, 1970

Hutt, Allen, *The problems of Editorial Display*. The Monotype Recorder 35, 1 (1936)

Lupton, Ellen, 'Historical Notes' in *Typographia polyglotta*. New York: Association Typographique Internationale and the Cooper Union, 1997

Milo, Thomas, 'Arabic script and typography: A brief historical overview' in *Language, Culture, Type, International Type Design in the Age of Unicode*, edited by John D. Berry. New York, NY: Graphis Press, 2002

Glossary of Terms

'Ajam: A word that refers to 'the other'; non-Arab.

Ascenders: Vertical strokes that extend above the x-height of a font.

Baseline: A line on which letters stand.

Counters: Any enclosed circular or curved white space present within letterforms.

Damma (ˀ): A diacritic mark on the top of any letter that creates the sound 'o' or 'u' after that letter.

Descenders: The portions of the letters that extend below the baseline.

Diwani: Literally 'chancery (or administrative) style'. A calligraphic style that was already in use at the 15th-century Ottoman administration (the *Diwan*), but which is certainly older.

Diwani Jali: Decorative Diwani.

Fatha (ˊ): A diacritic mark on top of any letter that creates the sound 'a' after that letter.

Fouss'ha: High standard Arabic; classic or modern Arabic.

Jazm: A diacritic mark on top of any consonantal letter that indicates that there is no vowel sound after that consonant. It's also known as *sokoon*.

Kashida: An elongation between connected characters; also used for justification.

Kasra ( ): A diacritic mark below any letter that creates the sound 'eh' after that letter.

Kerning: the horizontal space between two letters; it can be adjusted to balance the space between letters visually.

Khatt: Script or writing. *Fann al-khatt* is the art of writing, calligraphy.

Kufi/Kufic: An early angular, upright script and the first truly calligraphic style. It was the the second style used for Koranic text (the first and oldest style, with no calligraphic equivalent, is a slanted script called Hijazi).

Leading: The amount of space between lines of type, usually measured from the baseline.

Letterform: The shape of a letter; a glyph.

Ligature: Two or more Latin alphabet characters joined into a single character; common ligatures include 'ff' and 'Æ'; there are ligatures in Arabic.

Matrix: A mould used to cast a hot-metal letterform.

Monotype machine: A typesetting machine that casts characters in type metal as individual letters, and not as single lines.

Nabataean: Pre-Arabic script.

Naskh/Naskhi: A calligraphic style developed for copying manuscripts (*naskh* means 'to copy'), and is now the most widely used for body text setting.

PBUH (Peace Be Upon Him): A term of reverence that often follows the prophet Muhammad's name.

Riq'a/Rokaa: A bold calligraphic style mostly used in Egypt.

Sans serif: Any typeface or font with letterforms that do not use typographic projections and embellishments to complete a stroke of a letterform.

Semitic languages: The oldest family of related languages documented in written texts: Akkadian, Babylonian, Ugaritic, Phoenician, Hebrew, Aramaic, and Arabic.

Serif: Any typographic projection or embellishment that completes a stroke of a letterform.

Slug: A piece of type metal used to space paragraphs in typesetting.

Stylistic set: A feature of OpenType fonts; fonts with multiple alternate characters, such as ligatures and decorative swashes, can be grouped in stylistic sets so users know which alternate characters work well together.

Ta'jim: The adaptation of Arabic letters to represent sounds that are alien to Arabic speech.

Ta'liq: In the Persian tradition, this is the name of a precursor of Diwani (see above). In the Ottoman tradition, however, Ta'liq refers to a fluid calligraphic style with strong stroke contrast developed in early 15th-century Persia. This latter style is called Nasta'liq. In Arabic it's usually called Farsi 'Persian'.

Thuluth: A calligraphic style mostly used for inscriptions, titles, and headings. It is the sister script of Naskh (see above).

Tugra: The Ottoman imperial monogram with the name of the emperor.

X-height: The height of the letter x that defines the height of all lowercase letters, excluding ascenders and descenders.

Design Credits

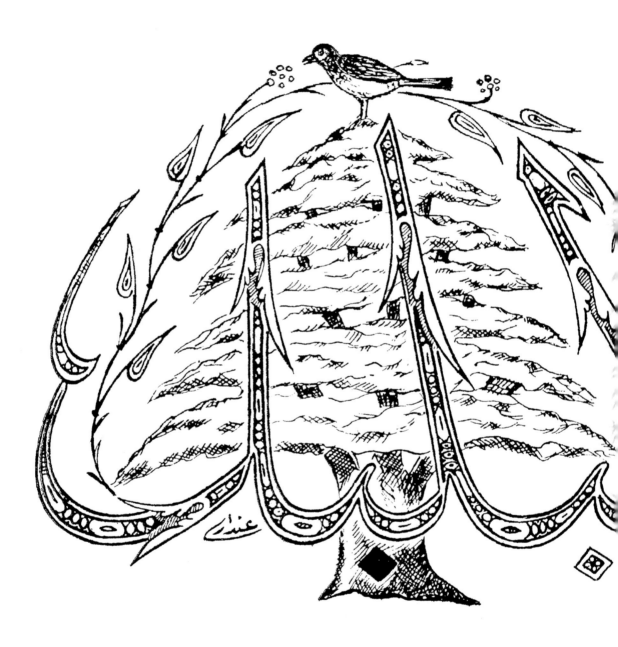

Calligraphy by Fahd Andari. The Arabic word *Al Bulbul*, meaning the nightingale, embraces the cedar tree, which is the symbol of Lebanon.

Tribute

Fahd Andari (1903–73) worked as a calligrapher, photographer, and teacher in Lebanon. Andari achieved great success and in 1934 was named an official calligrapher of the Lebanese Republic. He was one of only eighteen government authorized calligraphy and typography experts. He published several calligraphy textbooks that were adopted by schools in Lebanon. Most of his commercial work appeared on the pages of magazines and newspapers. One of his master works was the execution of forty-two words written on the silver cast of a sesame seed.

The following three individuals have greatly influenced contemporary Arabic calligraphy and typography:

- Thomas Milo developed the concepts of DecoType, together with his two partners Peter Somers and Mirjam Somers. DecoType is a font technology designed from the structure of the script, tweaking Arabic to adjust it to the limitations of technology, that takes into account both Arabic calligraphic tradition and modern aesthetic requirements.

- Walter Tracy designed the renowned typeface Times Europa. During the 1950s he and his team of experts designed Yakout, the most popular and most used typeface in Arabic desktop publishing.

- Mohamed Zakariya is an American-born Islamic calligrapher. He wrote *Music for the Eyes, An Introduction to Islamic and Ottoman Calligraphy*, the catalogue for the exhibition 'Letters in Gold: Ottoman Calligraphy from the Sakip Sabanci Collection, Istanbul'.

Mourad Boutros is acknowledged as one of the world's leading designers of Arabic typefaces and fonts. His company, Boutros, co-founded with his wife Arlette, has led the field of typography and calligraphy for more than forty years.

Martin Lambie-Nairn is a British designer, founder of the branding agency Lambie-Nairn, and the creative director of ML-N. His work has earned him numerous distinctions, including the D&AD President's Award and the Prince Philip Design Prize.

The author wishes to thank Halim Choueiry for his major contributions of art and insight.

The author also wishes to thank Ahmad Asfahani, Krikor Agopian, Bassam Andari, Marwan Aridi, Raymond Atallah, Waleed Al Asfar, Ian Bezer, Daniel Boutros, Mark Boutros, Gerry Ellender, Dave Farey, Martin Gibbs, Nebras Hameed, Andy Hayes, Cecil Hourani, Robert Jureidini, George Kandalaft, Father Elie Kesrouani, Nayla Lahoud, Martin Lambie-Nairn, David Learman, Ahmed Mallah, Nadim Matta, Thomas Milo, James Packer, Fadi Radi, Nigel Roche, John Rupert, Graham Spice, David Wadmore, Serge Zaccar, Mohamed Zakariya, Gregory Zuyen and others who may inadvertently have been missed for their contributions and advice.

Edited by Buzz Poole

Designed by Soulaf Khalifeh

This book is typeset in Tanseek Traditional

First published by Mark Batty Publisher as *Arabic for Designers* in 2007

This edition first published in 2017 in hardcover in the United States of America by Thames & Hudson Inc., 500 Fifth Avenue, New York, New York 10110

Arabic for Designers: An inspirational guide to Arabic culture and creativity
© 2017 Thames & Hudson Ltd, London

Text and images © 2017 Mourad and Arlette Boutros unless otherwise noted on page 221.

www.thameshudsonusa.com

Library of Congress Catalog Card Number 2016952915

ISBN 978-0-500-51953-0

Printed and bound in China by Reliance Printing (Shenzhen) Co. Ltd